Contents

Introduction

Collins Mental Maths is a series designed to help children develop effective strategies to carry out mental calculations and acquire a 'feel' for number.

The series is built around three beliefs:

- Being good at mental mathematics raises children's mathematical achievement considerably;
- Teachers can play a very important part in training children, by offering focused lessons, to develop the most efficient strategies for mental maths and acquire sound technical fluency;
- Mental mathematics can be planned so that, within an organised structure, it is possible to offer children enjoyment, challenge and success.

There are three teacher's guides in the series and they are designed to be used with children aged 5 to 7, 7 to 9 and 9 to 11 respectively, although many of the activities for one age range can easily be adapted for use with other age groups. The contents of the guides take into account the National Numeracy Framework, the requirements of the National Curriculum and the Scottish 5-14 Guidelines. Most of the ideas included in the teacher's books have been trialled by class teachers who have helped to select activities which are both motivating and practical.

All three teacher's guides have the same structure. Each one is divided into three sections.

Section 1 provides brief guidelines for teachers on aspects of good practice to bear in mind when teaching mental mathematics. Ideas for effective classroom organisation, pupil participation, differentiation, assessment and interactive displays are also included in this section.

Section 2 provides structured practical ideas for the teacher to use with the whole class or groups. Specific skills for the teacher to focus on are highlighted. These ideas can be used as 'ten minuteses', as part of the 'numeracy hour', or can be extended for use in the main teaching session. Ideas for extension are suggested so that some activities can also be used over a period of time. Possible learning and reinforcement outcomes are listed, along with ways of introducing the activities, questions, list of resources and extensions. Facing each teacher's page is a photocopiable activity sheet which relates to some of the skills addressed. The teacher's guide pages are cross-referenced to the pupil book pages.

Section 3 consists of more photocopiable activity sheets and games which children can use individually, in small groups or as part of a whole-class lesson. These sheets include activities which can be completed at the level specified by most children without much adult help. A collection of short puzzles and problem-solving activities are also included at the end of this section; these provide ideal opportunities for children to 'use' and 'apply' number. Many teachers have used these activities for whole-class teaching or for individual or pair work at the beginning or end of a lesson.

USING THIS GUIDE TO TEACH MENTAL MATHEMATICS

All the ideas here encourage children to be actively involved in mental calculations. Some activities are to be undertaken without the aid of paper and pencil, counters or any physical objects. Others involve recording or being engaged in activities which demand a great deal of mathematical thinking and estimating skills. Jotting down ideas is necessary on some occasions, where recording ideas helps children to extend their ideas further and be involved in higher levels of thinking and to internalise more complex ideas. Particular attention is given to encouraging children to construct mental images to help them acquire a conceptual understanding of mathematical ideas.

The collection of ideas on each of the teacher's pages is intended to be used over an extended period of time. Teachers may, of course, use the simpler ideas within an activity with a group of children and return to the more advanced aspects after a period of time. The photocopiable sheets provide some ideas for recording; again, these can be adapted for extended use. In selecting activities to be included in the book the following features were considered important:

- Motivating and meaningful contexts;
- Opportunties for practice and reinforcement;
- Possibilities for building mental imagery;
- Opportunities for oral work.

3

THE IMPORTANCE OF TEACHING MENTAL MATHEMATICS

The importance of children being able to do mental mathematics has always been recognised; the Cockcroft Report (1982), 'Mathematics 5-16' (HMI 1985) and the National Curriculum have all made strong recommendations that children should develop effective strategies for mental calculations. International comparisons of children's mathematical competencies and the National Numeracy Project have brought the role of mental mathematics to the forefront of mathematics education. Teachers recognise both the power children can derive from being 'good' at mental mathematics and their professional role in supporting children in achieving that objective. Everyone's ability at mental mathematics can be increased through structured activities and practice. This series offers guidance for that purpose.

Understanding concepts and being good at mental arithmetic go hand in hand in supporting each other. In order to encourage conceptual understanding of ideas which will enrich children's mental mathematics skills, the teacher needs to address the following:

- Provision of practical activities which help children to explore the nature and inter-relationships between numbers and of the number system.

- The use of number lines and structured materials to introduce and enhance children's understanding of concepts. The use of such materials should be to support children to develop mental imagery and strategies to work with numbers more effectively. Children should not be made to depend on them for longer than necessary.

- The need to be able to 'recall facts' – number bonds and table facts – quickly is effective and necessary, but understanding the principles behind these facts is also important. It makes it possible for children to tackle more complex applications of these facts by restructuring and adjusting what they know.

- The advantage of having short, regular mental maths sessions focusing on specific strategies. Without specific teaching, it is unlikely that children will develop the most efficient and economical methods of calculations. The use of 'child methods' may bring success in the short term; only systematic teaching is likely to make children develop effective strategies in the long term.

- The advantage of having regular sessions with specific emphasis on memorising facts.

DISCUSSION AND MENTAL MATHEMATICS

Effective teaching of mental mathematics will involve a considerable amount of oral work. Verbalising mathematical thinking enhances children's confidence. Listening to others makes them consider methods used by other people and their relative efficiency in order to refine their own thinking and methods.

Discussion during mental mathematics lessons may take many forms:

- The teacher introduces new ideas and demonstrates the ideas through clear explanations, inviting questions and clarifications from children. An interactive style of teaching will keep children actively involved in the learning process.

- Children are asked to share their methods, with the teacher structuring the discussions in such a way that all children's contributions are valued. These discussion can highlight the relative effectiveness of the methods used, encouraging children to develop sensible strategies.

  The types of questions which will elicit useful responses are: 'That was quick, tell me how you did it'; 'Can you tell everyone how you did it?'; 'If you were the teacher how would you explain it?'; 'Tell the person next to you how you did this'; 'That is great, I had never really thought about it that way' and so on.

  The sharing of methods can also be achieved through paired work. The children can ask each other mental maths problems and then probe how their partner tackled the calculations. They can then report back to the big group about the strategies used. Giving time to think before shouting out answers will help children to consider the 'reasonableness' of their responses and reflect on their methods.

- The quality of children's responses will most certainly depend on the type of questions asked. It is useful to remember that open-ended questions can bring a variety of answers which will help children to learn from each other.

- It is useful to discuss mistakes made by other 'imaginary' children in order to highlight misconceptions, errors and faulty strategies. For example, 'Daniel is working out 4 add 5 on the number line. He answered 8. Is the answer right? If not, what do you think Daniel might have done?'
  Responses may include that he probably started counting and included the 4: 4, 5, 6, 7, 8... and so on.

- The role of discussion in assessing children's learning is crucial. It is only through asking children probing questions and listening to their rationale for using different methods that the teacher can plan the children's future learning and evaluate their own teaching.

ORGANISING YOUR CLASS FOR MENTAL ARITHMETIC

Conducting effective mental mathematics lessons requires a great deal of thinking and planning which makes it one of the most challenging aspects of a teacher's work. The important issues to consider are Differentiation, Grouping and Creating a 'mental maths' environment in the classroom.

Differentiation

It is very likely that the 30 children in the class are at different stages in their mental mathematics development which makes differentiation an important aspect to consider. The following suggestions may help to achieve differentiation.

- When introducing an activity to the whole class, target the questions carefully so that some consideration is given to the children's level of ability to respond.
- Teach half or quarter of the class together for mental arithmetic whilst the other children work on a task introduced previously or something they can work on independently.
- Inviting children who put their hands up to respond is not always the most appropriate strategy. Ask children to keep their answers 'in their heads' until the teacher selects a person to answer a question.
- When asking for responses to the 'quick-fire' type of questions, encourage children to show their answers by holding up number cards when asked to do so. This enables the teacher to skim all the responses quickly.
- Encourage children to write down their answers individually as 'top secret' so the teacher can control how to deal with individual children's responses.
- Tell children to have some thinking time before responding.
- After the introduction to the activity get children to work in pairs or small groups with differentiated tasks. Extension ideas are provided in the teacher's guides.
- Use open-ended questions which will enable children to work at their level of ability.

Grouping

It makes sense to teach the whole group together when a new skill or idea is being introduced. For example, when the idea of doubling is introduced all children can be shown what it means. It also helps to tell children, in advance, what they are going to do and what is the purpose of an activity. The importance of listening to each other and the need to have a quiet time when everyone is thinking, should be stressed. Give children opportunities to participate in different roles according to their capability and talent; for demonstrating ideas, volunteering to be players, explaining activities, recording on the number line, for score keeping and so on.

Small group work will be more appropriate when it is felt that children need to discuss ideas more thoroughly and make decisions which need more thinking and reflection. Ability grouping may be more appropriate for some tasks. The teacher may want to be present in one focused group for assessment purposes.

Mental maths activities can also be done in pairs or individually. The activity sheets, games and puzzles included in this book can be used for any of the above grouping styles.

Creating a 'mental maths' environment in the classroom

In order to succeed in teaching mental mathematics, it needs to be given a high profile. The following ideas have been found useful by practising teachers:

- Have a mental maths lesson at least four times a week. Short, well paced and focused '10 minute' lessons are sufficient. Some of these lessons may be used to introduce new ideas and others may be for testing what has been learnt or a combination of both.
- Focus on learning selected facts for the week such as learning two number facts or number bonds. 'Tell someone about these bonds' or design a poster showing what the learnt number bonds mean.
- Have interactive displays in the classrooms. For example, put up a question: 'The answer is 20, what are the questions?', inviting children to put up their responses on strips of paper all week.
- Make 'counting times' special, using appropriate types of counting activities: rhymes, what number comes after 3, 29, 399 and so on.

- Have a regular 'close your eyes' time asking children to picture numbers, number lines, structured materials, calculations. Ask them to share what they see with others.
- Let children have their own number kits which contain number lines of different-sized numbers, blank lines for working things out, a collection of dice, sets of 0-9 number cards, their favourite number game and other materials useful at the time of teaching new ideas.
- Have a vocabulary book or display of useful words to learn and remember.

ASSESSING MATHEMATICAL LEARNING

Assessment of children's mental mathematics learning will normally be carried out by:

- listening to children's responses to direct questions, during discussions between the teacher and children or amongst children themselves;
- observing children working on tasks which require numerical recording;
- marking children's written responses to tasks on the pupil book pages.

The following questions will be useful to consider when assessing children's mental mathematics:

- Are children using the correct mathematical vocabulary?
- Can they recall useful number facts?
- Are they able to work accurately and with speed?
- Are they able to use taught strategies efficiently?
- Are there any misconceptions in pupils' understanding of ideas?

Diagnostic interviews with children will help to highlight the nature of any specific difficulties which can be dealt with.

STRATEGIES FOR DOING MENTAL ARITHMETIC

In general terms, the following strategies help to acquire competence in mental arithmetic:

- Instant recall of number facts.
- Using a fact from memory and making adjustments to use these facts in other situations.
- Rearranging numbers to make a calculation more manageable.

- Knowing doubles and halves.
- Using a mental number line.
- Using mental imagery developed through previous experiences.
- Estimating a possible solution.
- Splitting numbers into parts to make calculations easier.
- Using generalised rules of multiplying and dividing by 5s, 10s, 100s and 1000s.

Some helpful points for teachers using this guide

Many of the teaching points, strategies and ideas explored in this book are built on concepts introduced earlier in Teacher's Guides 1 and 2. As children need to practise basic skills, concepts and strategies regularly, it is highly recommended that the two earlier guides be referred to. Also, as children get older, differences in their attainment, experiences and understanding become wider. This makes it necessary for teachers to revisit concepts and ideas previously taught.

The main new ideas explored in this book are: strategies for working with decimals, number properties and skills such as divisibility and percentages. The central idea of place value, based on the fact that the value of a digit is determined by the position it occupies in a number, must continue to be on the main agenda because decimal numbers are built on the same principles. Any gaps in understanding or misconceptions about the principles of place value can be exposed through discussions. Activities using arrow cards (Book 2) are very useful resources for Years 5 and 6 both for reminding children of 'place value' as well as for extending the arrows to include thousands. A robust understanding of place value must still remain a priority at this stage.

Activities which involve decision-making, working in pairs, considering whether facts are reasonable and playing team games with the whole class are particularly suitable for this age group to support children to internalise sound, mathematical ideas. Practising basic mental calculations and number bonds must also be a regular feature of maths lessons.

Addition of three or more numbers

RESOURCES

One set of three dartboards (Resource master 1), counters

KEY LANGUAGE

add, times, how many more, totals, double, re-order, partition, rounding

REFERENCES

Pupil Book 5: pages 2, 4, 5, 6, 11
Pupil Book 6: pages 10, 11, 17, 18

LEARNING OUTCOMES

- Practising addition of three or more numbers.
- Reinforcing a variety of strategies for adding numbers.
- Finding differences and doubling.
- Multiplication.

TEACHING NOTES

- Introduce children to one of the dartboards and explain what the regions mean for scoring. If, for example, a dart is placed in the 'double 4' region, it is worth 8; a 'treble 8' scores 24 and a 'quadruple 9' scores 36.
- Ask: 'If you are free to place three darts in any region, what is the highest score you can get?' On dartboard number 1, it is 24. (Place all three darts on 'double 4'.) Say to the children: 'Using dartboard number 1, how many ways can you score 13?' There are lots of ways, such as $d3 + d3 + 1 = 13$; $d4 + 3 + 2 = 13$. Let children contribute their ways of scoring 13 in turn.
- Using dartboard number 2, ask the children to get a score of 53. Say: 'What is the highest/lowest score you can make with three darts on dartboard number 3?' Get the whole class to help you to tabulate all the possible scores on a board or flip chart for dartboard number 2. By phrasing a variety of questions within this motivating context, children can be encouraged to carry out addition, multiplication and finding differences mentally.
- Use this context of having to add a string of numbers to revisit and reinforce the following strategies:
  – Re-ordering: When adding numbers, put the larger number/s first or group numbers in order to make the addition process easier. For example, first look for numbers adding up to multiples of ten. When adding a string of numbers: $36 + 21 + 14 + 22 + 19$, it is easier to add 36 and 14 first ($36 + 14 = 50$), and then $21 + 19 = 40$ and then add $50 + 40 + 22 = 112$ to get the total.
  – Partitioning: Splitting into hundreds, tens and units and adding them separately. To add $54 + 68$, add $50 + 60 = 110$ and then $4 + 8 = 12$ to make the total $110 + 12 = 122$.
  – Doubling and finding near doubles such as $27 + 25 = 52$. Doubling 25 is 50, then add 2.
- Give children bigger numbers to add mentally, using the most suitable strategies discussed in the context of the dartboards.

EXTENSION ACTIVITIES

- Increase the number of darts used.
- Design a dartboard game with clear rules.

Hops to the target

Jump to the target number in 4 hops using addition, subtraction or multiplication.
Some numbers are already filled in.

The first one has been done for you.

1.

2.

3.

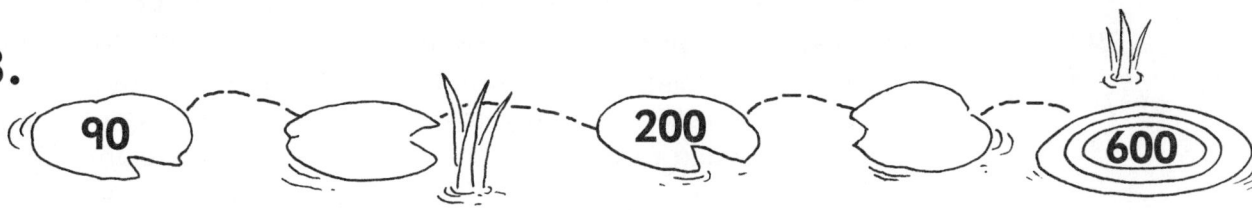

4.

5.

On the back of this sheet, make up some more
'4 hops to the target' for your friends to complete.

Name _____   **Date** _____

Collins Mental Maths © HarperCollins Publishers Ltd 1998

Number sequences

RESOURCES
Number lines,
matchsticks, cubes

KEY LANGUAGE
pattern, sequence,
next, series, predict,
rule

REFERENCES
Pupil Book 5:
pages 3, 29
Pupil Book 6:
pages 3, 4, 5

LEARNING OUTCOMES

- Using mental arithmetic to work out number patterns and sequences.
- Predicting numbers in a sequence and working out rules.
- Working out number sequences using whole, decimal and negative number lines.

TEACHING NOTES

- Remind children of their earlier experience (Teacher's Guide 2) of making number patterns, predicting sequences and explaining the rules. Get children to come to the front of the class and make up a number sequence, say 6, 8, 10, 12. Meanwhile, the others work out the rule used to build up the sequence. When someone calls out 'stop', let the person say what the next number is and how it has been arrived at. Ask: 'What is the rule applied by the sequence-building person?' Select different children to make the most challenging number sequences they can manage for others to work out.
- At this stage, it is useful to choose contexts such as square numbers, multiples and cube numbers for making up sequences. This provides children with an understanding of how numbers grow following a rule. It also involves them in 'figuring out' large numbers needed to work out the sequences for square and cube numbers. For example, ask children to make a series of squares and say: 'What is the next number in the sequence?' 'Can you predict what will be the tenth in the series? 4, 9, 16…'
- Let a volunteer make the next two terms in the series below. Ask them to explain how the series builds up: 3 + 1; 5 + 3 + 1; 7 + 5 + 3 + 1 and so on. Ask: 'Can you close your eyes and tell me how many cubes are needed for the model of the 5th term?' 'If you are given 160 cubes, how tall will the model be?' In order to tackle the last question, children will need to look at the total number of cubes and notice that each model is made up of a square number – 4, 9, 16 and so on. 160 cubes will build a tower 12 cubes tall and there will be some cubes left over.

- Use decimal and negative number lines and mixed operations to build up number sequences. Ask the children to work out the rules.

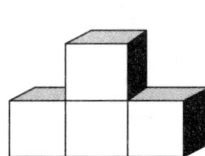

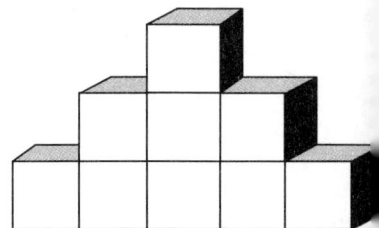

EXTENSION ACTIVITIES

- Let children generalise a rule for predicting the 10th and 20th numbers in sequences and justify the rule.

Sequence trails

In each of the following number trails, the numbers are in a special sequence.
Work out the sequences and fill in the blank circles.

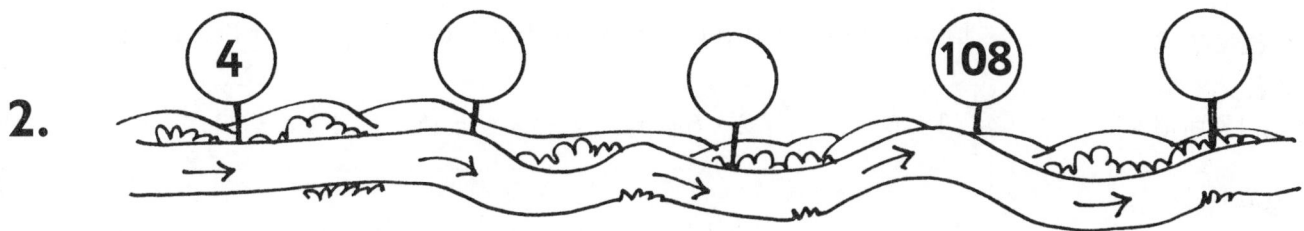

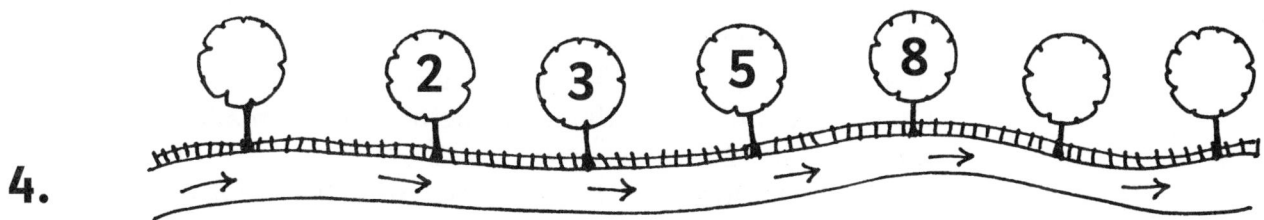

1. (4) (8) (16) (32) ( ) ( )

2. (4) ( ) ( ) (108) ( )

3. (7) ( ) (42) (168) ( )

4. ( ) (2) (3) (5) (8) ( ) ( )

5. (1024) (512) (256) ( ) ( )

Name _____ **Date** _____

Relations

RESOURCES

Multiplication table for the number 6 written on cards, multiplication cards for checking purposes

KEY LANGUAGE

multiply, divide, add, subtract, double, half, same, inverse, decimal, check

REFERENCES

Pupil Book 6: pages 17 and 28

LEARNING OUTCOMES

- The use of known multiplication facts to generate other related facts.
- Reinforcement of the relationship between multiplication and division.
- Commutativity of multiplication.

Focused teaching of these points will encourage children to find alternate mental strategies and develop an effective checking mechanism.

TEACHING NOTES

On a board or flip chart, write the following multiplication facts:

| 1 x 6 = 6 | 2 x 6 = 12 | 3 x 6 = 18 | 4 x 6 = 24 | 10 x 6 = 60 |

- Say to the children: 'If you don't know the answer to 16 x 6, which of these cards will help you to find the answer?' The children could then explain their reasons for choosing the appropriate cards. Ask further similar questions.
- Look at a multiplication fact with the children, for example, 8 x 6 = 48. Ask them: 'What is 6 x 8? 16 x 12?' Often, children will respond to 16 x 12, recognising that it is double 48. This is a useful discussion point.
- Ask the children: 'What other facts can you derive from the fact that 8 x 6 = 48?'
- Move on to other related facts which are useful when calculating mentally. 'If 12 x 13 = 156, what is 156 ÷ 12? 156 ÷ 13?' For some children it is useful to demonstrate this using smaller numbers, for example, 2 x 4 = 8 so 8 ÷ 4 = 2.
- Say to the children: 'If 8 x 6 = 48, what is 80 x 60? 800 x 600? 8000 x 6000?' Ask several children for their responses. A common mistake with the first question is to respond with the answer 480.
- For children who have been introduced to dividing by 10 and 100 and decimal points, discuss further related facts which can be derived: 8 x 0·6 = 4·8, 0·8 x 0·6 = 0·48.
- Give pairs of children a multiplication fact and ask them to list all the related facts they can derive from it.

EXTENSION ACTIVITIES

- The children could make up a multiple choice questionnaire to test someone's knowledge of related facts.
- Organise a display of challenging related facts for a multiplication fact.

Number machines

Remind yourself about the relationship between multiplication and division.
Now fill in the missing numbers and signs on these machines.
The first one has been done for you.

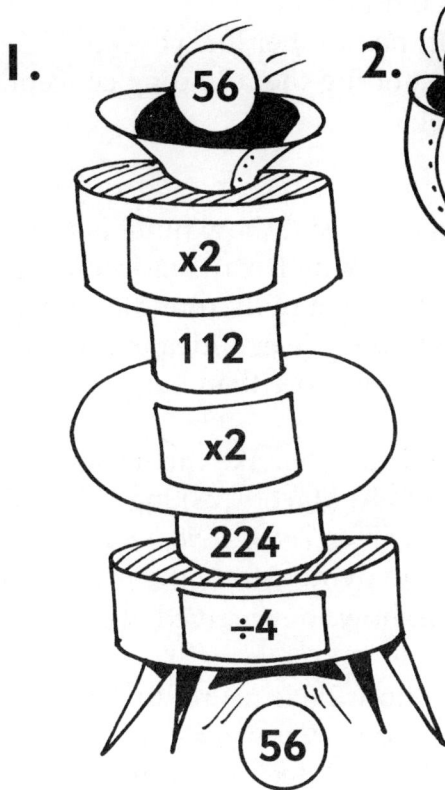

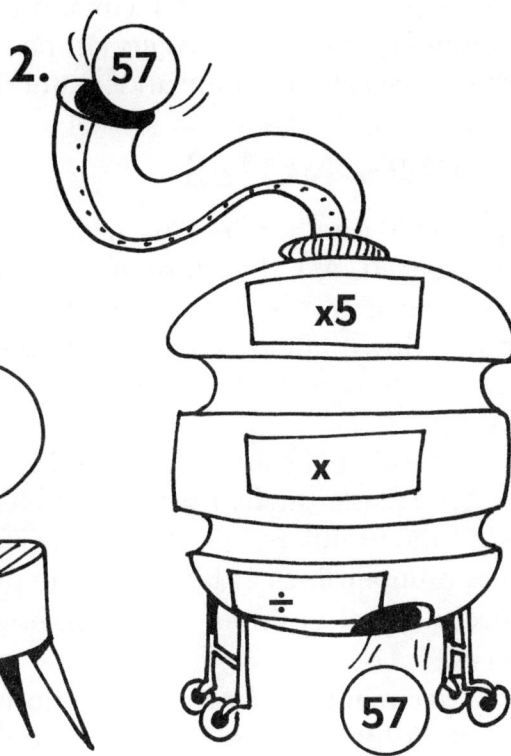

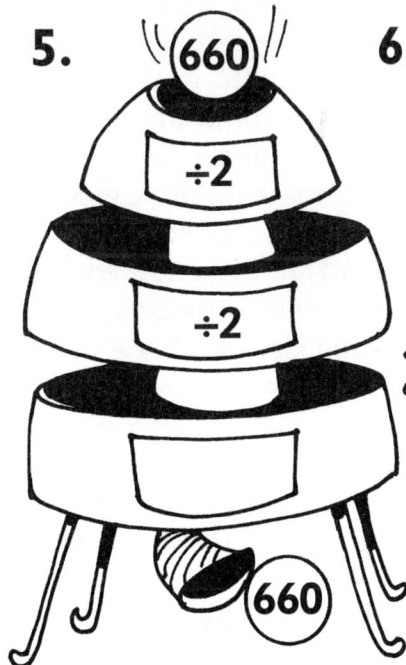

1.

56
x2
112
x2
224
÷4
56

2.

57
x5
x
÷
57

3.

64
÷8
x
64

4.

8
x25
÷
8

5.

660
÷2
÷2
660

6.

300
÷
÷
x12
300

Name _____   Date _____

Rounding

RESOURCES

Whole and decimal number lines, blank number lines, sum cards with addition and subtraction sums

KEY LANGUAGE

round up or down, nearest ten, hundred and thousand, nearest whole number, distance

REFERENCES

Pupil Book 5: pages 8, 9
Pupil Book 6: pages 2, 3

LEARNING OUTCOMES

- Reinforcing and practising the concept of rounding numbers.
- Using the 'rounding' strategy for adding and subtracting numbers.
- Introduction to rounding of decimal numbers.
- Development of mental imagery of the number line concept which is a useful model for understanding the rounding concept.

TEACHING NOTES

- Using a 0-100 number line, discuss the idea of how numbers are equally spaced. Ask the children to show half-way marks on the number line as this is the deciding factor in both 'rounding up' or 'rounding down'. Reinforce the previously learnt idea that under half-way you 'round down'; half-way or more than half-way, you 'round up'.
- Practise the idea of rounding up or down to make the nearest 10, 100 or 1000 using the half-way principle. Start by asking children to round the numbers 348, 891, 6004, 6790, 7983, 4658, 98 765. Use parts of number lines or blank lines to demonstrate the process. It is useful to ask children to explain how they arrived at the answers.
- Using a decimal number line, show how 2·6 is nearer to 3, so you round up; 5·4 is nearer to 5, so you round down.
- Ask children to close their eyes and round decimal numbers up or down using a mental number line. Suggest that they round these numbers to the nearest whole number: 2·6, 6·5, 9·8, 45·8. Extend the idea to two decimal places.
- Relate the rounding strategy to measures and ask questions involving kilometres, metres, centimetres, litres, millilitres, kilograms and grams where the concept can be used in a meaningful context.
- Remind children how the idea of rounding can be used to make addition and subtraction easier. This idea should be familiar to children (see Teacher's Guide 2) and it can now be used to do operations with larger numbers and decimal numbers. For example, $84 - 19 = 65$, $84 - 20 = 64$, $64 + 1 = 65$, $243 + 88 = 331$ $(243 + 90) - 2 = 331$; $(4·5 + 4·7) = (4·5 + 5) - 0·3 = 9·2$. Encourage children to explain the process of breaking down the sums. Practise regularly to help children to grasp these ideas.

EXTENSION ACTIVITIES

- Write addition and subtraction sums on cards and ask groups of children to work them out. Draw the whole class together to discuss the rounding strategies.
- Get children to work with larger numbers and numbers with two and three decimal places using the rounding strategy.

Rounding luck

Alan, Shanti, Winston and Melanie each chose a set of cards with eight numbers written on them. The teacher called out eight numbers in order and asked them to round their numbers up or down in the same order.

The person who had the nearest number each time, circled that number.

The person with the most numbers circled, won the game.

Who was the winner?

_____

Teacher's numbers

120	270	50
500	300	17
1000	8	

Alan's numbers

97	259	50·3
472	290	15·9
899	7·2	

Shanti's numbers

104	269	42·9
509	308	16·8
998	7·4	

Winston's numbers

109	282	39·9
489	297	18·7
1200	7·8	

Melanie's numbers

117	263	59
469	291	18.2
1111	8·7	

Name _____ **Date** _____

Doubling and halving

RESOURCES

Sets of 'Where is it?' cards (Resource master 2 photocopied and enlarged)

KEY LANGUAGE

double, halve, add, subtract, twice, multiply, divide

REFERENCES

Pupil Book 5: pages 4, 5, 16-18, 20, 21
Pupil Book 6: pages 9, 17-20

LEARNING OUTCOMES

- Reinforcement of doubling and halving of whole numbers.
- Introducing doubling and halving strategies for carrying out calculations which involve a fraction.
- Carrying out mental calculations faster to facilitate instant recall.

TEACHING NOTES

- Remind children about the different strategies they have been introduced to previously for doubling and halving numbers, including the idea of finding near doubles. As a warm up to the activity, ask some quick-fire questions to double the numbers 34, 56, 340, 256 and so on. The strategy children use for doubling 34 may be different to doubling 56 which crosses over the 'ten', so it is useful to discuss different strategies used. Ask how they would add the numbers 256 + 257 making use of the 'near doubles' strategy of doubling 256 and adding 1 to get the answer. Follow these with questions which involve larger numbers: double 3250, halve 9200, add 8900, 8700 and so on.
- Explain to the children that they are going to use the doubling and halving strategies – some will involve fractions. Ask: 'What is double 39? half of 90? half of 97? twice 700 and a half? What is 675 the half of?' Explain that when doubling bigger numbers, it may be useful to split the number into H, T, U. For example, to double 364 it may be easier to double each place value first:
  double 364 = 600 + 120 + 8 = 728
  double 2345 = 4000 + 600 + 80 + 10 = 4690
- Using the cards on the Resource master, play the game 'Where is it?' with the whole class. The last card loops back to the first card – this will mark the end of the game. Explain the rules to the children. The first child reads the front of the card: 'I am 130, where is double me?' the child who has the card 260 will call out 'I am 260, where is add 16?' This will be answered by the child who has the number 276. Keep playing until all the cards are used up. The game can be played with any number of children and is a useful way to practise mixed operations.

EXTENSION ACTIVITIES

- Play 'Where is it?' using larger numbers and more advanced operations including square or cube numbers and decimals.
- Get children to make up sets of cards for different sizes of groups.

Mysteries

I am thinking of a number. If I double it and add 30, the answer is 84.
What is my number?
You can work it out by taking away 30 from 84 and halving the result.
This gives my number: 27.

Double 27 = 54 + 30 = 84

Find these mystery numbers.

1.   I am thinking of a number.
      If I double it and take away 18, I get the answer 58.
      What is my number? _____

2.   I am thinking of a number.
      If I halve it and halve it again, I get the answer 190.
      What is my number? _____

3.   I am thinking of a number.
      If I take away 900 from it and halve it, the answer is 605.
      What is my number? _____

4.   I am thinking of a number.
      If I double it and double it again, the answer is 1100.
      What is my number? _____

Make up some more mystery numbers on the back of this sheet.

FINISH

START

Name _____   **Date** _____

Highs and lows

RESOURCES

0-9 number cards, two sets of place-value boards marked with decimal points, one marked with tens, units and tenths and another with tens, units, tenths and hundredths:

H	T	U	$\frac{1}{10}$	$\frac{1}{100}$
		•		

KEY LANGUAGE

decimal point, value, higher, lower, tenth, hundredth, whole numbers, nearness

REFERENCES

Pupil Book 5: pages 3, 13, 14
Pupil Book 6: pages 2, 3, 14, 15, 16

LEARNING OUTCOMES

- Development of the concept of the decimal point and its importance in place values, through discussion and imagery building.
- Ordering decimal numbers.
- The concept of approximation and rounding off.

TEACHING NOTES

- Discuss how the size of numbers is determined by the position occupied by digits. Ask children to explain why the number 7543 is larger than 7345. Stress the importance of the positional aspect and how values of digits get larger as they move to positions on the left.
- Place a digit card, say 6, on the tens position on the place-value board. Ask: 'What is the value of this digit? Can you describe it in terms of cakes? What does it look like?' Highlight the idea that it actually stands for 60 whole cakes. Now move the digit 6 to the units position. Ask the children to describe the size of the digit 6, now representing only 6 single cakes.
- Place the digit 6 in the column marked 'Tenth' on the board and ask children to describe its size. Draw out the idea that the '6' in the 'Tenth' column is only six tenths which is, in fact, less than one whole cake. Move the digit 6 to the Hundredth position to show that it now represents six hundredths of a cake, emphasising the reduction of the size. Draw attention to how the movement to the right mirrors the movement to the left.
- Introduce the game 'Highs and lows' by selecting two players to demonstrate the rules to the whole class.
- Give each player a set of 0-9 number cards and a place-value board marked with H, T, U, Tenth and Hundredth. Children should choose either 'highest' or 'lowest' as their criteria for making numbers before the game starts.
- Each player turns up the top card and places it in a position on the board bearing in mind the criteria selected. Once the card is placed it cannot be moved. The other four cards are placed in the same way. The winner is the player who makes the number which fulfils the criteria. Encourage children to verbalise their

EXTENSION ACTIVITIES

- Use boards which include 'Thousandth'.
- Suggest that the children make up dominoes and snap cards to show different ways of expressing fractions and decimals.

Reduce to zero

Jane reduced the numbers 475 and 52·56 to zero, digit by digit, using her calculator.

To reduce 475 she pressed:
>   −70 and got 405
>   −5 and got 400
>   −400 got 0

To reduce the decimal number 52·56 she pressed:
>   −2 and got 50·56
>   −0·5 and got 50·06
>   −0·06 and got 50
>   −50 and got 0

Imagine you are using a calculator. Show how you would reduce the following numbers digit by digit by subtraction. Record the keys you would press and what the display would show.

When you have worked out the methods, check each one on a calculator.

1. 653

2. 4398

3. 45·6

4. 46·78

5. 457·89

Name ....   **Date** ....

Fractions and decimals

RESOURCES

Visual aid of whole and parts of chocolate bars (Resource master 3), two dice, one marked 1, 2, 3, 4, 5, 6 and the other marked 0·1, 0·3, 0·5, 0·7, 0·6 and 0·8 (dice can be marked appropriately for particular levels as required)

KEY LANGUAGE

digits, value, decimals, fraction, tenths, whole-number difference, add, total

REFERENCES

Pupil Book 5: pages 3, 12, 13, 14
Pupil Book 6: pages 2, 3, 14, 15, 16, 29, 29

LEARNING OUTCOMES

- Reinforcement of the structure of decimal numbers.
- Highlighting the relationship between fractions and decimals.
- Development of mental strategies for adding and subtracting decimal numbers.

TEACHING NOTES

- Remind children about decimal numbers being related to fractions, tenths, hundredths and so on, which would have been taught previously. Illustrate the 'tenths' idea using visual aids of whole and decimal representations of chocolates. Ask: 'What does this piece stand for?' If the answer is 0·2, say: 'What should be added to 0·2 to make a whole one?' 'What if you add 0·4, what do you have now?' 'How could you make a whole one?' Then, without using visual aids, ask the children to close their eyes and imagine: 'You have two whole bars of chocolate. I give you 0·3 more and then another 0·5. Open your eyes and tell me what you have altogether. What do you need to make three whole bars of chocolate?'

- Get three volunteer players to illustrate the decimal target game. The objective of the game is to make the target number using dice throws. Say the target is 3 (3 whole ones). Each player in turn throws the decimal die and records the running total. If player A throws 0·3 first, then 0·5 followed by 0·7 the total is 1·5. The player still needs another 1.5 to get to the target. Emphasise the difference aspect by asking: 'What does player A need to get to the target?' Change to larger targets 10, 20, 50 and so on by playing two dice together.

SCORE SHEET
Player A
0·5 + 0·5
0·8 + 0·7
2·5

- The reverse of the game can be used for practising subtraction of decimals – you could call this game: 'Racing to zero'. The target is zero each time. Let all the players start with a whole number, say 6. Play the decimal die to subtract the decimal numbers and keep a running record. For example, if player A starts with 6 and throws 0·5, 0·7 and 0·1, after three throws the score is 4·7. Play both dice for racing to zero from larger numbers. The first person to reach zero or less wins.

- Follow this game with quick-fire decimal addition and subtraction questions.

EXTENSION ACTIVITIES

- Play the game using different numbers on the dice and extend to hundredths.
- Get children to make up 'snap' games using different representations of decimals: fractions and pictures of decimals.

Decimal trails

On this decimal trail Sam, an adventurer, will win £30.00 because his exit total is larger than the winning total marked at the end of the trail.

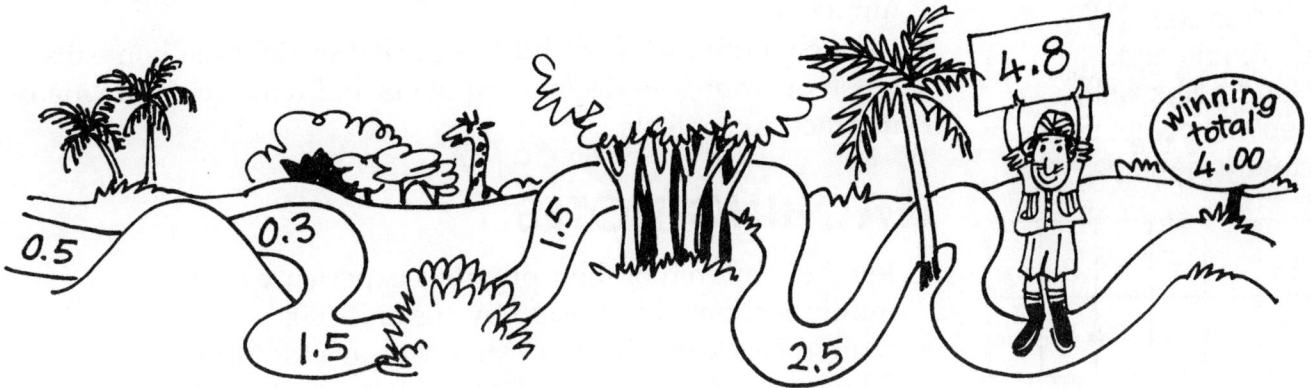

Complete the table and tick the box to show which adventurers will win £30.00.

Name of adventurer	Trail numbers to follow	Adventurer's exit total	Winning total
ANNIE	0·5 + 0·3 + 1·5 + 2·5	4·8	4·0
HANNAH	1·5 + 0·5 + 2·00 − 0·5		4·1
AHMED	1·00 − 0·8 + 4·2 + 0·7 + 0·4		5·3
ARIF	0·6 + 3·4 − 0·9 − 0·3		3
BILLY	2·03 + 1·3 + 0·56 + 4·0		6
GILROY	0·9 + 0·9 + 0·9 − 1·2		5·98
ASHA	1·25 + 2·5 + 3·4 − 2·00		5

Name .... **Date** ....

Collins Mental Maths © HarperCollins Publishers Ltd 1998

Decimal 'shifts'

RESOURCES

Place-value boards marked with Th, H, T, U, Tenths and Hundredths with decimal points very clearly marked:

Th	H	T	U	$\frac{1}{10}$	$\frac{1}{100}$

dice marked x10, x10, x100 and ÷10, ÷10, ÷100, sets of 0-9 number cards, calculators

KEY LANGUAGE

places, values, tenths, hundredths, move, shifts, decimal point

REFERENCES

Pupil Book 5:
pages 24, 25
Pupil Book 6:
pages 23, 27, 28

LEARNING OUTCOMES

- Extending multiplication and division by 10 and 100 to decimal numbers.
- Understanding what a 'shift' to the left or right really means when operating on decimal numbers and reinforcing the ideas in practical contexts.

TEACHING NOTES

- Remind children of their previous experiences with multiplication and division by 10s and 100s.
- Using place-value boards, demonstrate and discuss the movement to the right and left. Ask a volunteer to come to the front of the class and show number 34 on the place-value board. Now multiply that number by 10, then by 100, showing the movement to the left making that number 340 and 3400 respectively. Ask the children to explain how the values change to hundreds and thousands when multiplying.
- Now show the process of dividing by 10s and 100s, again by demonstrating on the place-value board. Show how 34 divided by 10 becomes 3·4 and 34 divided by 100 becomes 0·34 by moving to the right. Emphasise that when this is done without the board, the decimal point appears to move to the left. When multiplying whole numbers by 10 and 100 the 'adding zeros' rule needs to be explained here, very carefully, to show that 3·4 x 10 does not actually result in 3·40!
- Use a calculator as a visual aid to show the shifts in digits. Let children input a number on to the calculator. Call out 'multiply' or 'divide' by 10s and 100s. Let the children predict what the calculator will show before pressing the keys.
- Play the decimal game. Use three volunteer players to demonstrate the game. You will need the dice marked x10, etc. Choose a two-digit number and ask each player to write it on to their score sheet. This is the starting number. Decide how many turns to have before the game starts. In turn, players throw the dice, operate on the number and keep a record of the total. If the starting number is 54 and a player throws the dice four times, say x10, ÷100, x10, x10, the recorded scores will be 540 followed by 5·40, 54 and 540. Compare the results to see who ends up with the highest number.

EXTENSION ACTIVITIES

- Extend the activities and the game to multiplying and dividing by thousands.
- Ask children to design a track game which involves multiplying and dividing whole and decimal numbers by 10s, 100s and 1000s.

Jammed

A decimal machine which multiplies and divides by 10s and 100s, is jammed and can't print the output numbers. Fill in the output numbers.

MULTIPLY BY 10

Input	Output
3·4	34
8·9	
0·7	
1·2	
11·3	
12·62	
61·73	

DIVIDE BY 10

Input	Output
3·7	0·37
36·1	
170	
21·89	
0·76	
1·99	
2·06	

MULTIPLY BY 100

Input	Output
3·7	
1·3	
7·78	
6·2	
8·76	
0·83	
10·76	

DIVIDE BY 100

Input	Output
4·76	
53·6	
4·63	
0·98	
10·05	
43·00	
6·9	

Name _____ **Date** _____

Divisibility rules

RESOURCES

Appropriate cards with suitable numbers on them which are to be used for discussion Have a collection of cards with square numbers, and so on, and numbers to illustrate the divisibility rules

KEY LANGUAGE

factors, multiple, prime numbers, square numbers, divisible, remainder

REFERENCES

Pupil Book 5:
pages 27, 28, 29
Pupil Book 6:
pages 4, 5, 22

LEARNING OUTCOMES

- Revisiting the idea of multiples, factors, prime numbers and square numbers previously learnt.
- Introducing 'divisibility' rules which help to carry out speedy factorisation of numbers without having to go through laborious calculations.
- Offering the divisibility rule as a useful checking mechanism when dividing numbers.

TEACHING NOTES

- Remind children of the idea of factors and prime numbers which they should be familiar with. Ask them to list all the factors of 36: 1, 2, 3, 4, 6, 9, 12, 18, 36. Ask them to factorise 19: only 1 and 19. Using these examples, discuss the ideas of factors and prime numbers.
- Ask: 'What are square numbers?' 'What is the largest square number you know?' 'What is its square root?' Get the whole class to recite the square numbers 1 to 20 working them out mentally. Can a square number be a prime number? Ask for the reasons for their response.
- Ask the children: 'Was 1900 a leap year? How do you know? We can tell by dividing by 4 and if there is no remainder it was a leap year.' 'Do you think 1900 is divisible by 4?' After responses are given, test them to find out. It was not a leap year, although some children may say that it looks like a leap year. 'What about 2010? Will that be a leap year?' Use this context to introduce the divisibility test.
- Using examples, explain the divisibility rules. A number is:
  Divisible by 2 if the last digit is even
  Divisible by 3 if the sum of the digits is divisible by 3
  Divisible by 4 if the last 2 digits are divisible by 4
  Divisible by 5 if the last digit is 0 or 5
  Divisible by 6 if the number is even and is divisible by 3
  Divisible by 9 if the sum of the digits is divisible by 9
  Divisible by 8 if the last 3 digits are divisible by 8
- Let pairs or groups of children choose one of the rules and carry out quick mental checks to see whether these rules really work.
- Hold up cards with reasonably large numbers and ask children to list the factors of the numbers.

EXTENSION ACTIVITIES

- Ask children to try multiples of 11 and invent a rule for testing divisibility by 11. This can be done by adding both sets of alternate digits in a number and finding the difference between the totals. If the difference is 0 or 11 the number is divisible by 11. For example, in the number 453 233: 4 + 3 + 3 = 10 and 5 + 2 + 3 = 10, so the number is divisible by 11.

The culprit

1. A mathematics professor was an eye-witness to a bank robbery. Everything happened very quickly, but she was able to remember the number on the robber's T-shirt. When she got home, she wrote the number down. She also wrote down some clues about the number. She then gave the clues to her maths students to see if they could work out the number.
Can you work out the number from the following clues?

- It is an odd number.
- It has 4 digits.
- It is divisible by both 3 and 9.
- When it is divided by 21 there is no remainder.
- All the digits are different.
- The total of the first two digits is double the total of the last two digits.
- The number is between 2999 and 5000.

The number is _____.

2. Here is another 'mystery' number. Can you work it out from the following clues?

- The number is between 7500 and 9900.
- It is divisible by 6.
- All the four digits are different.
- It is a square number.

3. Using ideas of divisibility, square numbers, multiples, factors and other ideas, make up some clues for the following numbers.
Ask your friends to detect them.

97   345   3948   676   2401   4848

Name _____ **Date** _____

Multiplication

RESOURCES

A set of cards with multiplication sums such as 52 x 7; 38 x 5; 67 x 6 written on them, sets of 0-9 number cards

KEY LANGUAGE

times, multiply, partitioning, splitting

REFERENCES

Pupil Book 5: pages 22, 23
Pupil Book 6: pages 25, 26

LEARNING OUTCOMES

- Reinforcement of multiplication tables.
- Practise in multiplying by tens.
- Understanding that when multiplying a two-digit number by a single-digit number, it is useful to multiply the tens first and then the units. This way of splitting/partitioning calculations into manageable parts is a good point to stress for undertaking all calculations.

TEACHING NOTES

- Explain to the children that they are going to look at an efficient way of multiplying two-digit numbers by a single-digit number; by splitting them into parts.
- Ask some quick-fire multiplication questions: 5 x 7; 8 x 6; 9 x 4 and so on.
- Practise the ten times table with the whole class working out: 7 x 30. It may be necessary to demonstrate what it means, 30, 60, 90... (7 times) to 210.
- Ask children to think about how they would work out 67 x 6. It is likely that some children will offer the strategy of doing it as a formal sum. Say: 'Can you think of any other ways of doing this?' If no one offers the partitioning method, show how this can be done. It can be done as 60 x 6 = 360 and add this to 7 x 6 = 42 providing the answer 402. This lesson will be an opportunity to also show the use of brackets: 67 x 6 = (60 x 6) + (7 x 6) = 402.
- Using the multiplication sum cards, practise the partitioning method of multiplication with the whole class. Invite the children to write the 'splitting up' way of doing it on the board or flip chart.
- Give the children a few sums cards and ask pairs of children to work out the sums. When tackling a card, one child can work out the tens and the other, the units. When working out 36 x 4, for example, child number one works out 30 x 4 and child number two works out 6 x 4. They then add the two results together to get the answer. Take turns to multiply tens and units.

EXTENSION ACTIVITIES

- Let children think of ways of using the same 'splitting' principle to multiply numbers with three and four digits and with decimals.
- Get children to choose three cards, say the cards of 4, 5 and 7 and ask small groups to make up the multiplication sum which gives them the highest result. Let them explain their solutions. For example, using the three cards you could make up different sums such as 45 x 7; 54 x 7; 74 x 5 and so on.

Fast times

Choose one number from Box A and Box B and multiply them in your head. Fill in the blank spaces so that each sum is correct. You can use the numbers more than once. The first one has been done for you.

BOX A

27   99   63   39

37   69   56   47

48   77   83

BOX B

3   4   7   6   8

9   5   2

69 x 3 = 207

99 x ☐ = 495

☐ x ☐ = 135

☐ x 8 = 552

☐ x 9 = 567

☐ x ☐ = 581

☐ x ☐ = 188

☐ x ☐ = 336

83 x ☐ = 498

☐ x 7 = 392

☐ x 8 = 296

☐ x ☐ = 351

☐ x ☐ = 693

Name _____   Date _____

Division

RESOURCES
Sets of cards with division sums such as 64 ÷ 8; 54 ÷ 6; 96 ÷ 6; 96 ÷ 16 extending to examples of larger numbers to be used

KEY LANGUAGE
divide, multiply, partition, factors, split, halve

REFERENCES
Pupil Book 5:
pages 15, 24
Pupil Book 6:
pages 21, 22, 28

LEARNING OUTCOMES

- Reinforcement of multiplication tables and the idea that division and multiplication are related operations.
- Carrying out division in the head by using a variety of methods: partitioning, halving and using factors.

TEACHING NOTES

- Ask children to divide a two-digit number by a single digit number, say 56 ÷ 8 and establish that they remember that 56 ÷ 8 = 7 and 7 x 8 = 56. It is useful to remind children that this works with numbers of any size and is one of the best ways of dividing in the head. Also stress, by using other examples on the board, that this offers an effective checking mechanism.
- They are now going to use some other methods which make division in the head easier to manage. Ask children to divide 68 by 4 and encourage them to discuss different strategies used. Suggest 'breaking' numbers into tens and units as another way of carrying out the division. For example, 68 ÷ 4 can be thought of as (60 ÷ 4) + (8 ÷ 4) = 17. Suggest other examples which involve carrying over: 56 ÷ 6 (50 ÷ 6) + (6 ÷ 6) first carry out 50 ÷ 6 which gives you 8 and 3 left over which has to be added to 6 within the second bracket. 8 ÷ 6 gives you 1 and 2 left over, which leaves the answer 9 and 2 left over. This way of partitioning will also help children to acquire a better understanding of the operation of division.
- Ask children to explain what 'factors' are, stressing the division aspect involved. Introduce 'dividing numbers using factors' as another method of carrying out mental division. Carrying out the division sum 64 ÷ 8 is the same as dividing by 4 and then dividing by 2. To do 112 ÷ 16, divide by 2, then by 4 and then by 2 again. This is a useful strategy to illustrate.
- Ask children to divide 96 by 8. A variety of strategies will be offered. Introduce them to the idea that in order to divide by an even number such as 8, an efficient method is to halve it (48), halve it again to obtain (24). Halving it further will give you the answer (12).
- It is useful to go over the different methods used for two reasons: firstly it offers a variety of strategies for dividing in the head; secondly, it provides explanations as to what the process of division involves.

EXTENSION ACTIVITIES

- Give division cards with larger numbers to small groups of children and ask them to think of the easiest strategy to carry out each of the sums.
- Ask children to explore how these ideas can be used with decimal numbers.

Division check

Michelle did some division sums very quickly in her head. Check the answers in 10 minutes. Mark them as P if they are possibly right and W if they are wildly wrong.

1.	96 ÷ 8	
2.	2500 ÷ 10	
3.	128 ÷ 6	
4.	360 ÷ 12	
5.	781 ÷ 9	
6.	560 ÷ 10	
7.	0·5 ÷ 2	
8.	306 ÷ 15	
9.	255 ÷ 15	
10.	4100 ÷ 100	

Answers

1.	12
2.	25 r 10
3.	21 r 2
4.	400
5.	908
6.	5·6
7.	0·25
8.	20 r 6
9.	17
10.	410

Name _____ **Date** _____

Money, time and measures

RESOURCES

Visual aids for concepts to be targeted such as weights, packaged foods with labels, tape measures, maps with scales written on them, newspapers, TV programmes, catalogues

KEY LANGUAGE

time, days, months, hours, minutes, seconds, kilometre, metre, centimetre, millimetre, kilogram, grams, litres, millilitres

REFERENCES

Pupil Book 5: pages 31, 32
Pupil Book 6: pages 31, 32

LEARNING OUTCOMES

- Mental calculations involving units of money, length, weight and capacity through meaningful contexts.
- Conversions of units.
- Estimating measures through application and by developing visual images.

TEACHING NOTES

- The purpose of the lesson is to make units of measurement and related calculations meaningful to children. Start the lesson by seeing if children know the basic facts. Ask them questions such as: 'How many minutes are there in an hour? How many grams in 4.5 kilograms? millimetres in 2 kilometres?'
- Suggest that the children play the game 'Likely or unlikely'. The children have to decide whether a statement made by the teacher or other children is reasonable by thinking about the statements, visualising and by carrying out some mental calculations.
- Start with the first statement: 'You have been alive for between 2000 and 4000 days.' Give children time to think, calculate and reason before selecting children to say whether the statement is 'likely' or 'unlikely'. Children must also give a reason for their choice. It may be necessary to have items available for checking the responses. Rough estimates are acceptable when calculations involve larger numbers.
- The type and content of the questions will depend on what is being targeted in the lesson, but examples of questions are: 'A car travels at a speed of 1500 km per hour in the town centre.' 'Your maths book weighs 1.2 kg.' 'I drank 360 millilitres of lemonade in one swallow.' 'There are 16 hours of children's programmes a day on BBC2.' 'The perimeter of a square playing field with sides 320 metres is 1280 metres.' 'There are 86 400 minutes in a day.' 'Anne can cycle 180 kilometres in 10 minutes.' 'Your height is about 240 metres.' 'You have been alive more than a million seconds.'
- Calculations involving money can be set in the context of exchanges for currencies abroad. Ask the children to convert the cost of items (for example, hamburgers, sports shoes, T-shirts) into British equivalents using exchange tables.
- Give children a page from a catalogue with some items marked. Ask them to work out whether 'Emma can afford to buy all the ticked items on the page for £500.00.'

EXTENSION ACTIVITIES

- Use statements which involve more challenging calculations for checking to see if the statements are reasonable.
- Let children make up their own 'likely' or 'unlikely' statements for mental maths sessions.

Best fit

There are seven statements on this page. For each statement, you have three options to choose from. Circle the option which is the best fit to the statement.

1. In three hours, a car travelled:
   a. 90 kilometres
   b. 9000 kilometres
   c. 2500 kilometres

2. The weight of a piano is about:
   a. 45 kilograms
   b. 450 kilograms
   c. 3600 grams

3. I have £45·00. This is enough to:
   a. buy 16 ball pens which cost £3·50 each
   b. buy 16 pantomime tickets for £2·95 each
   c. buy an electronic game costing £48·00 reduced by 10%

4. To save £1620, an employee saving £40·50 each week will have to save for:
   a. 100 weeks
   b. 40 weeks
   c. 50 weeks

5. A year is about:
   a. 8800 hours
   b. 2450 hours
   c. 30 000 hours

6. The internal angles of a regular hexagon are:
   a. 60°
   b. 75°
   c. 120°

7. You have £5.00. This is enough to buy some hamburgers at 83p each. You are able to:
   a. Buy 10 hamburgers
   b. Buy 6 hamburgers
   c. Buy 5 hamburgers

Name _____   **Date** _____

Place value of larger numbers

RESOURCES

Sets of 0-9 number cards, dice marked hundred thousands, ten thousands, thousands, hundreds, tens and units, playing board stencils for each player:

HT	T	Th	H	T	U

KEY LANGUAGE

thousands, hundreds, tens, units, place value, highest, lowest

REFERENCES

Pupil Book 5: pages 9, 25, 26
Pupil Book 6: pages 2, 3, 12, 13, 23

LEARNING OUTCOMES

- Identifying place values in larger numbers.
- Comparison of sizes of whole numbers with up to six digits.

TEACHING NOTES

- Explain to the children that they are going to play a game which involves making and comparing large numbers. Remind them how the place names H, T and U extend to the left in the same pattern as thousands, ten thousands, hundred thousands.
- Write some six-digit numbers on the board, including some with zeros as place holders. Ask the children to read them correctly. Write a set of six-digit numbers – 302 298, 300 953, 390 000, 339 999 – and ask the children to place them in order of size. Encourage the children to verbalise the strategies that they use.
- Invite three volunteer players to demonstrate how to play a game. The players decide whether the 'highest' or 'lowest' score wins the game before commencing. Each player selects a card from the set of shuffled 0-9 number cards which is placed face down on a table. They then throw the dice and record the selected digit in that position. For example, if player A picks up the number card 4 and gets the dice throw of 'Ten thousands' he or she writes the 4 in the 'Ten thousands' place. If the dice throw place has already been filled, the player misses a turn. Players take turns until one person has filled all the places. The others then fill their empty places with zeros.
- Compare the size of the numbers. The player with the highest number wins. Choose 'lowest' to be the next round's winner. Encourage children to explain how they decide which is the highest/lowest number.
- The game can be played in small groups with the dice appropriately marked with 3, 4, 5 or 6 places.

EXTENSION ACTIVITIES

- Extend the board to include decimal places.
- Ask children to imagine they have won £100 000. How would they spend the money? Suggest that they show money calculations adding up to the total amount.

Treasure search

This grid shows a map of a site where some treasure is buried. The treasure diggers have marked in pounds (£) the value of what is buried underneath each square unit.

Which of the three routes should they follow in order to get the largest amount of treasure? Mark the route they should take by going over it with a red pencil.
They can only move in right angles, as shown on the map.

£............		£............	
£2005	£10 300	£4200	£1001
£90	£1990	£9835	£85
£100	£19 108	£1000	£4080
Start	£2000	£26 230	£761

£............

Name _____ Date _____

Collins Mental Maths © HarperCollins Publishers Ltd 1998

'Fast' multiplying

RESOURCES

The connect grid written on a board or flipchart (Resource master 4), colour chalks or board pens, calculators for the referees

KEY LANGUAGE

multiply, times, divide, estimate, product, factors, multiples

REFERENCES

Pupil Book 5: pages 15, 21, 22, 23, 26, 27
Pupil Book 6: pages 4, 5, 17, 20, 21, 23, 24, 25

LEARNING OUTCOMES

- Practise 'fast' multiplying two numbers using a variety of methods and learning new strategies.
- The relationship between the processes of multiplying and dividing.
- Estimating.
- Revision of previously taught mental strategies.

TEACHING NOTES

- It is best to play this as a class team game first in order to facilitate discussion and sharing of strategies. Divide the class into two teams and explain that they are allowed discussion time before offering their responses.
- Each team takes it in turns to 'claim' a number on the grid. They then say which two numbers in the box, when multiplied, will give that product. If the other team accept the claim, the number is marked with a team colour or a counter is placed on that number. If the claim is challenged then the referee is asked to check it on the calculator. The object is to claim four numbers in a row – horizontally, vertically or diagonally.
- It is important to ask questions periodically while the game is being played. Ask: 'How did you work that out?' 'How did you know that those numbers will give that product?' 'Why did you go for that number first?' Children are likely to use the following strategies: by looking at the last digits of the numbers in the grid and seeing which numbers in the box would give that product; by working it out from knowing what the factors are; by doing a quick estimate of how many times a number in the box would go into a number on the grid and by using known number facts.
- After the game, ask children if they have learnt anything new – number facts or new strategies – from the game.
- Send children away to play the game in groups. You could ask them to make a list of new ideas which can be brought back to the whole class after the game. The 'connect' game idea can be usefully employed to practise any mental strategies: addition, subtraction, multiplication and division or a mixture of these by designing particular types of grids.

EXTENSION ACTIVITIES

- Use more challenging grids and larger numbers, decimals and fractions.
- Let children make up a variety of grids which would involve them in doing the mental arithmetic themselves.

Broken keys

Imagine that the ⑦ key on your calculator is broken. If you were asked to use a calculator to do these sums, how would you do them?
Write down your methods as shown in this example:

27 x 9   26 x 9 = 234 + 9 = 243

1.
58 x
7
___

2. 71 + 397 =

3. 73 x 16 =

4. 852 ÷ 7

5. 426 – 37

6. 137 more than 663

7. 482 less than 700

8. 70 x 70

Name _____   **Date** _____

Properties of number

RESOURCES
Small sheets of paper and pencils, 0-100 number lines, parts of number lines and blank number lines

KEY LANGUAGE
larger than, smaller than, between, multiples, square numbers, cube numbers, prime numbers

REFERENCES
Pupil Book 5: page 7

LEARNING OUTCOMES

- Developing a 'feel' for number.
- Opportunities to consider the nature of large numbers.
- Ordering whole numbers, negative numbers and decimals by exploring the number line.
- Reinforcing properties of number.

TEACHING NOTES

- This activity has high potential for helping children to develop a 'feel' for most aspects of number. It can be adapted for use in different contexts and can be repeated many times throughout the year.
- Display a 0-100 number line where everyone can see it. Ask a volunteer to come to the front of the class and write a number between 1 and 100, in 'top secret', on a piece of paper (say, 67). The rest of the class then decide how many questions they need to ask to find out the secret number. You might decide that the children can ask the volunteer only 10 questions. The volunteer can only respond with 'yes' or 'no'. Select children who have questions to ask, providing enough time for others to think and eliminate the 'no' numbers. Likely questions at the early stages are: 'Is it bigger than 50? Is it an even number? Is it a prime number, multiple of…?' and so on. With practice, the nature of the questions will improve. Encourage discussion of strategies and discourage wild questioning without listening to responses to previous questions.
- This time, choose a decimal number. Provide blank number lines for children to refer to. The secret number is between 3 and 10 (say, 3·6). Questions could include: 'Is it bigger than 4? less than 3?' (No to both questions.) This suggests a decimal number. 'Has it more than three digits?' 'Is its value less than three and a half?' Allow a reasonable number of questions. Reduce the number of questions allowed when strategies to guess improve.
- When using larger numbers for this activity, it is necessary to give children two or more clues at the start, depending on the objective of the activity. For example, 'My secret number is between 2000 and 2900. It is an odd number and a square number.' (In this case 2500, which is the square of 50.)
- Use negative 'secret' numbers.

EXTENSION ACTIVITIES

- Use larger secret numbers.
- Organise an interactive display of secret numbers outside the classroom where other children can pin up their guesses.

Number quiz

Try this number quiz in the shortest time possible.

1. Using the digits 1, 3, 6 and 7 once only in each number, write down all the numbers bigger than 3600 from the largest to the smallest.

_____

2. Find all the numbers between 100 and 200 which can be divided by 19.

_____

3. Find six numbers between 1000 and 12 500 which are multiples of 29.

_____

4. Find two consecutive numbers which, multiplied together, give you 1722.

_____

5. What is the largest number between 500 and 1250 that is a multiple of 2, 3, 4, 5, 6 and 8?

_____

6. I have the same number of 20p coins and 50p coins in my pocket. The total amount I have is £15·40. How many coins do I have?

_____

7. Write down all the multiples of 39 you can think of in 2 minutes.

_____

_____

Name _____   **Date** _____

Percentages

RESOURCES

Pictures of items that will appeal to children – including topical ones – from catalogues and price tags marked: 10% off, 6% off, 40% off and so on. A large percentage/fraction number line for mental calculation practice and whole-class discussion

KEY LANGUAGE

percentage, fraction, discount, reduction, decrease, equivalent, profit, loss

REFERENCES

Pupil Book 6: page 2

LEARNING OUTCOMES

- Reinforcement of the understanding of percentages.
- Understanding of the relationship between fractions and percentages.
- Calculating percentages mentally.

TEACHING NOTES

- Discuss the number line below marked with fractions between 0 and 1. Then consider the number line showing percentages which lies parallel. Ask the children to come to the front of the class and show the approximate positions of 20%, 5%, 33%, 6%, 18% and others on the percentage number line.

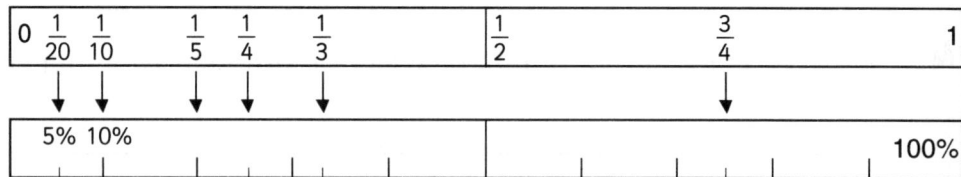

- Once the connection between fractions and percentages has been established, ask the children to work out the new prices of selected items from the catalogues or pictures. Introduce different percentage reductions using the price tags. 'What is the reduction in the price of a bat marked 30% off, a cuddly toy marked 20% off, 6% off a Walkman, a bicycle marked 11% off?' and so on. Discuss how the new prices are worked out.
- Suggest that the children imagine they have won £50/£100/£200 in a competition. What items would they choose? Say 'You have to work these out mentally, as you would have to in a shop.' Ask the children to explain their choices.
- Send children away to choose items worth higher amounts and work out the discounted amounts mentally. They can jot down the prices of individual items for the purpose of totalling only.

EXTENSION ACTIVITIES

- Use more catalogue examples of percentage reductions which are of increasing challenge.
- Ask the children to search for real examples – in school or at home – of percentage reductions of prices of cars and other items advertised in newspapers. Make a display with the examples.
- Ask questions such as: 'Would you rather have 30% of £40 or three fifths of £40; a third of 210 sweets or a quarter of 300 sweets...' and so on.

Grubo's Fast Foods

This is the menu in the window of Grubo's Fast Foods.
There is a holiday discount, so all prices are reduced.

MENU
Pizza per piece 80p
French Fries 68p
Chicken Bites £1
Burger 96p
Coffee 60p
Cola 40p
Lemon Fizz 40p
Ice-cream 50p

HOLIDAY DISCOUNTS:
30% off all drinks
12% off Chicken Bites
5% off Pizza
25% off Fries
33% off Burgers

Matthew, Hassan, Natalie and Asha do some mental calculations
of what their choices will cost. Each of them has £3.00 to spend.
Here are their choices:

MATTHEW
1 Chicken Bites
1 Fries
1 Ice-cream
2 Colas
Total =

HASSAN
2 Pieces of pizza
2 Fries
1 Lemon Fizz
1 Ice-cream
Total =

NATALIE
1 Burger
1 Pizza
2 Fries
1 Cola
Total =

ASHA
2 Burgers
2 Fries
1 Coffee
1 Ice-cream
Total =

Work out mentally how much each person
would have to spend. Add the total to
each list.

Who can't afford to order their
chosen foods?

Name _____   **Date** _____

Mental arithmetic strategies

RESOURCES

Two cards, one marked A and the other marked B for pairs of children. Choose appropriate sums as required.

A'S CARD

152 + 38

26 – 8

139 x 17

B'S CARD

258 + 39

28 – 6

118 x 11

KEY LANGUAGE

add, subtract, multiply, divide (and related vocabulary according to strategies used)

REFERENCES

Pupil Books 5 and 6: A and B cards are suitable for discussing most topics in both pupil books

LEARNING OUTCOMES

- Discussing, sharing and modifying mental arithmetic strategies.
- Carrying out mental calculations in addition, subtraction, multiplication and division.

TEACHING NOTES

- Tell children that the purpose of this activity is to carry out mental calculations in their heads using the most efficient ways. They then share their strategies with their partners and with the whole class. Ask some warm-up questions: 'Add 56 and 49, subtract 48 from 90.' Probe the children to illustrate how they, in turn, can probe their partners later.
- Give out the A and B cards to pairs of children and ask them to be A or B, as the card indicates. They take it in turns to ask each other questions. No paper and pencil are allowed for calculations. A asks B to carry out the first calculation within a reasonable amount of time. When B gives an answer A asks B to explain how he or she did the sum. A makes notes of how B did the sum, because A will have to share B's strategy with the rest of the class later. Ask them to reverse roles. Allow a reasonable amount of time for completing the tasks.
- Children come back as a whole class. Select one particular sum, say subtraction, and record all the different methods suggested by the children. Allow time for reflection, as it is likely that children will be fascinated by a more effective way offered by a classmate and will need time to assimilate this. It is important to accept children's own strategies, however, as they need to be offered alternate models for adoption if they wish.
- The lesson can be concluded by asking children to close their eyes and think about what was discussed in the lesson. Ask: 'Is there anything in particular that interested you today about subtraction?'

EXTENSION ACTIVITIES

- Ask children to make posters of how one sum (for example, division by 17) was done by different people and display all the methods.
- Use A and B cards for operations with decimals and fractions.

Digits search

There are some digits missing in these sums.
Work out what they are and write them in the blank boxes.

1. 18 x ☐ ☐ = 324

2. 397 – ☐ ☐ = 368

3. 2006 – ☐ ☐ = 1974

4. 437 x ☐ + 137 = 1448

5. 19 x ☐ ☐ = 228

6. 36 x ☐ x ☐ = 540

7. 65 + ☐ 99 = 664

8. 600 ÷ ☐ ☐ = 24

9. 2·5 x ☐ = 5

10. 2·3 x ☐ = 6·9

Name --- **Date** -------------------------

Collins Mental Maths © HarperCollins *Publishers* Ltd 1998

Resource master 1

1.

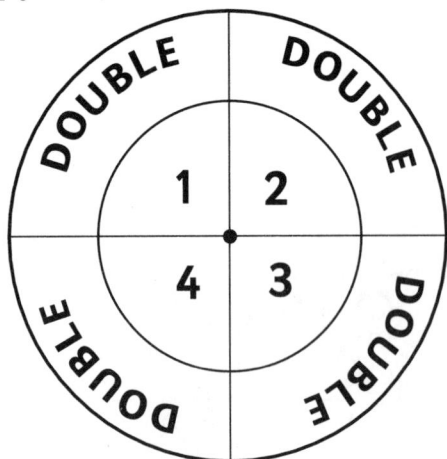

2.

3.

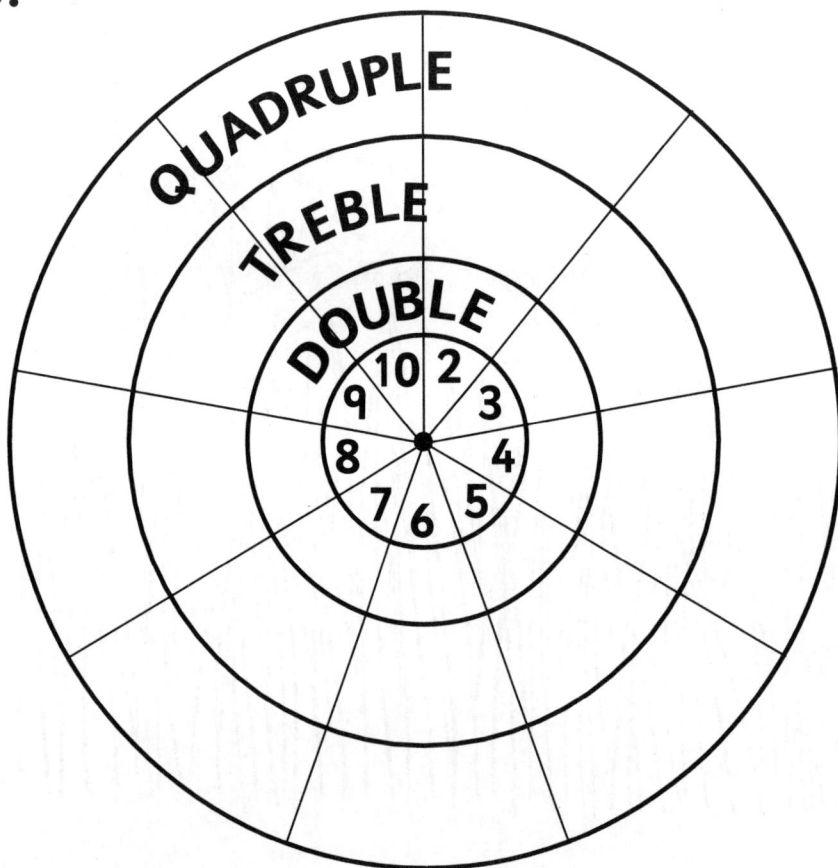

Resource master 2

DOUBLING AND HALVING (page 18)

I am 130, where is double me?	I am 260, where is add 16?	I am 276, where is half of me?	I am 138, where is add 72?
I am 210, where is double me twice?	I am 840, where is take away 60?	I am 780, where is add 10 and then halve me?	I am 395, where is add 25?
I am 420, where is times 3 of me?	I am 1260, where is 2500 take away me?	I am 1240, where is half of me?	I am 620, where is half of me?
I am 310, where is times 3 of me?	I am 930, where is a fifth of me?	I am 186, where is double me?	I am 372, where is double me?
I am 744, where is take away 614?			

Resource master 3

FRACTIONS AND DECIMALS (page 22)

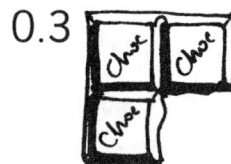

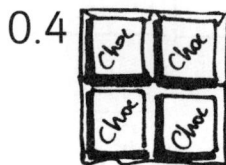

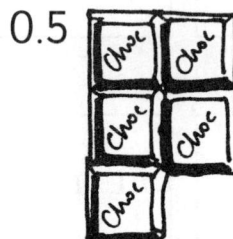

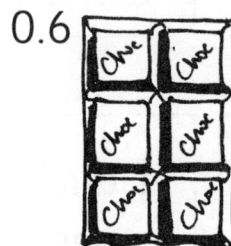

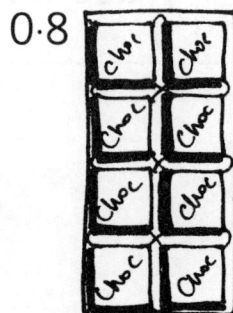

0.1

0.2

0.3

0.4

0.5

0.6

0.7

0.8

0.9

Resource master 4

'FAST' MULTIPLYING (page 36)

133	189	551	1349	1197	756
252	732	441	756	189	147
1827	57	21	427	1281	87
147	3843	4331	203	1159	609
213	183	2059	1769	441	551
36	399	497	84	348	1323

3	7	12	29	71
21	63	61	19	

Activities, games and puzzles

In this section more activities, games and puzzles are provided. The primary objectives of this section are to encourage children to:

- practise their mental arithmetic skills;
- provide meaningful contexts for carrying out mental calculations and appreciating the importance of mental recall;
- be involved in mathematical thinking and reasoning;
- realise the role of systematic work in mathematics;
- be involved in oral communication of mental mathematics.

The activities in this section are designed to be used by children without much adult help. It would be helpful, however, if children read the instructions with an adult present who can make sure they understand what is to be done. It is hoped that the games will be played many times and that the teacher will adapt the ideas to suit different groups of children and use them in other contexts. The puzzles on pages 49-59 are suitable for individual or class work. They are intended to be worked on for short periods of time and be returned to, if necessary, for further work. Some of the puzzles are quite challenging and solving them should develop children's confidence and persistence.

Mathematical games provide teachers with ideal opportunities for assessment; for observing children and for listening to them in natural and relaxed contexts. Points to look for:

- Are children using mental recall where they can?
- Are they using the most effective strategies available to them?
- Are they developing their mental fluency and 'feel' for number?

Finally, it is good to remember that in order to produce the best mathematicians, we need to attend to their personal qualities. Children need to enjoy mathematics and feel willing to 'have a go'. This section should support that mission.

Amazing

Fill in the squares below, using the following digits once only.

1 2 3 4 5 6 7 8 9

Here is an example: $\boxed{1}\ \boxed{2}\ \boxed{6}$ + $\boxed{3}\ \boxed{5}\ \boxed{4}$ = 480

1. Make the largest possible answer.

$\boxed{}\ \boxed{}\ \boxed{}$ + $\boxed{}\ \boxed{}\ \boxed{}$ =

2. Make the smallest possible answer.

$\boxed{}\ \boxed{}\ \boxed{}$ − $\boxed{}\ \boxed{}\ \boxed{}$ =

3. Make the largest possible answer.

$\boxed{}\ \boxed{}\ \boxed{}$ x $\boxed{}\ \boxed{}$ =

4. Make the smallest possible answer.

$\boxed{}\ \boxed{}\ \boxed{}$ ÷ $\boxed{}$ =

5. Make the largest possible answer.

$\boxed{}\ \boxed{}\ \boxed{}$ + $\boxed{}$ =

6. Make the smallest possible answer.

$\boxed{}\ \boxed{}\ \boxed{}$ x $\boxed{}$ =

7. Make a three-digit square number.

$\boxed{}\ \boxed{}\ \boxed{}$ x $\boxed{}$ =

Name _____   **Date** _____

Cross number

Fill in the cross number puzzle. Use a pencil
in case you need to change your entries.

Across	Down
a. The square of 12	**a.** 84 + 32
c. Half of 76	**b.** 4786 to the nearest 10
e. Double 137	**c.** The cube of 7
g. Treble 213	**d.** 20% of 3620
h. Two dozen	**e.** 286 − 52
i. 1·4 x 100	**f.** 200 km in miles
l. 75% of 320	**i.** 75 miles in km
n. 756 − 384	**j.** 29 x 8
p. 78 x 9	**k.** 25 squared
q. $\sqrt{625}$	**m.** The largest prime between 40 and 50
	o. The number of hours in 3 days

Design a cross number puzzle

Here is a blank cross number grid. Make up some challenging clues to go with it.
You may want to write some numbers down in the grid first and then work out the
clues.

Across	Down
a. _____	**a.** _____
c. _____	**b.** _____
f. _____	**d.** _____
g. _____	**e.** _____
h. _____	**f.** _____
k. _____	**i.** _____
l. _____	**j.** _____
n. _____	**m.** _____
o. _____	

Name _____ **Date** _____

Quick match

Pick a number from the box and match it to the description.

961	8100	1001	130
	756	1800	

1. It is a square number between 800 and 1000.

_____

2. If you add 3 consecutive numbers you get this answer.

_____

3. 90 squared is this number.

_____

4. Add a half of 260 to itself and divide it by 3.

_____

5. A multiple of 7, 11 and 13.

_____

6. You get this answer when you multiply two consecutive numbers.

_____

Name _____   **Date** _____

Collect your factors

A game for 2 players

You need: a set of 1-50 number cards

- Arrange the cards in rows showing 1 to 10, 11 to 20, 21 to 30, 31 to 40 and 41 to 50.
- Player A chooses a card from any row and places it face up. This card now belongs to A. Player B studies the card and takes and keeps all the cards which are factors of the number on the card.
- Now it is player B's turn to choose a card. B chooses his or her card from the collection and places it face up. A can now take all the cards from the collection which are factors of the card B has chosen. The game finishes when both players agree that there are no cards left which have factors.
- Here is an example: Player A selects the card 21 from the pile. This is A's card. B picks up 3 and 7 from the pile and keeps them. Number 1 is not allowed as a factor. Now it is B's turn to pick a card, say, card 24. Player A can take 2, 3, 4, 6, 8 and 12 from the pile and keep them.

It is worth thinking about some clever strategies to limit the number of cards taken by your partner!

Name _____ **Date** _____

Relatives

A game for 2–3 players

You need: a copy of the numbers below, a different-coloured pen for each player and a calculator to check answers in case of disagreement

- The aim of the game is to find relatives by looking for pairs of numbers and connecting them with an arrow.
- The rule for joining two numbers is to double a number and add on one. For example, 34 can be joined on to 69 because 69 is double 34 + 1.
- Keep joining pairs, in turn, until you cannot find any more pairs to join.
- The person with the largest pairs of relatives at the end of the game, wins.
- Now make up another board with numbers which can be relations. Some ideas for relations are: halve and take away 2, times 15, is a quarter of, and so on.

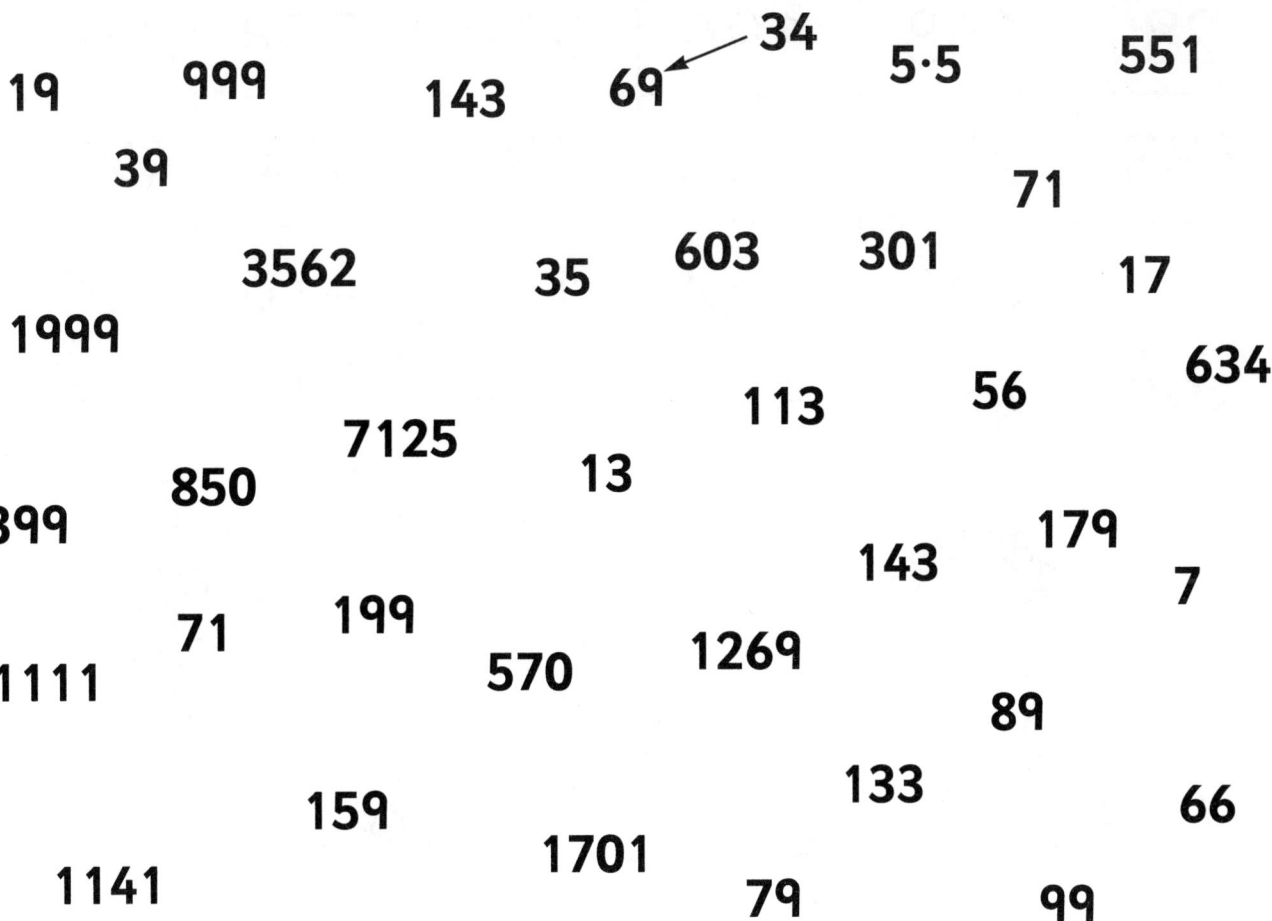

19   999   143   69 ← 34   5·5   551

39   71

3562   35   603   301   17

1999   634

113   56

7125   13

850   179

399   143   7

71   199

1111   570   1269

89

159   133   66

1141   1701   79   99

Name ------------------------------   **Date** --------------------------

28 table search

A game for 2 or more people

You need: a grid each with the times-table bonds for 28, pencil and paper

- First of all, decide how long you are going to play the game for.
- Study the grid and record as many 28 times-table bonds as you can find. Record each one like this: 3 x 28 =

Scoring system

For bonds up to 28 x 4 (5 points each)
For bonds from 28 x 5 to 28 x 8 (7 points each)
For bonds higher than 28 x 8 (10 points each)

28	168	196	224	308	336
588	252	56	280	84	420
112	364	532	140	476	504
392	448	560	56	616	644

Name _____   **Date** _____

Decimal connect

A game for 2–3 players

You need: different-coloured counters – one colour for each player,
a copy of the grid below

- Take turns to select a number on the grid.
- Choose two numbers, one from the circle and one from the rectangle
  and multiply them to give a number on the grid.
- If the calculation is accepted as correct by the other players, cover the grid
  number with a counter.
  (In case of disagreement use a calculator to check the answer.)

The aim is to get four counters in a line, horizontally, vertically or diagonally to score
a point. Keep playing until all possible spaces are covered.

0·3	25	21·09	0·84	300	2
14·06	60	1·92	20	6	0·04
1	35·15	2·4	0·1	500	12
0·6	3	20	50	800	4·8
1·68	8·4	0·8	2·8	4·921	1·2
70	70·3	0·72	49·21	1	56·24

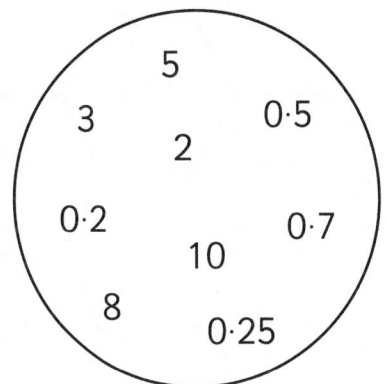

Circle:

	5	
3		0·5
	2	
0·2		0·7
	10	
8		
	0·25	

Rectangle:

12	1·5
1·2	0·2
100	0·25
2·4	4
7·03	0·5

Name _____   **Date** _____

Get a line

A game for 3–4 players

You need: counters of different colours, one colour for each person and a copy of the grid below

- Each player takes turns to choose a number from the grid.
  The players then choose two numbers from box A and box B which,
  when added together or subtracted, give the chosen number.
- If the answer is correct, the player places a counter in the hexagon.
  If there is disagreement, check the sums with a calculator.
- The winner is the first one to get a whole row of counters.

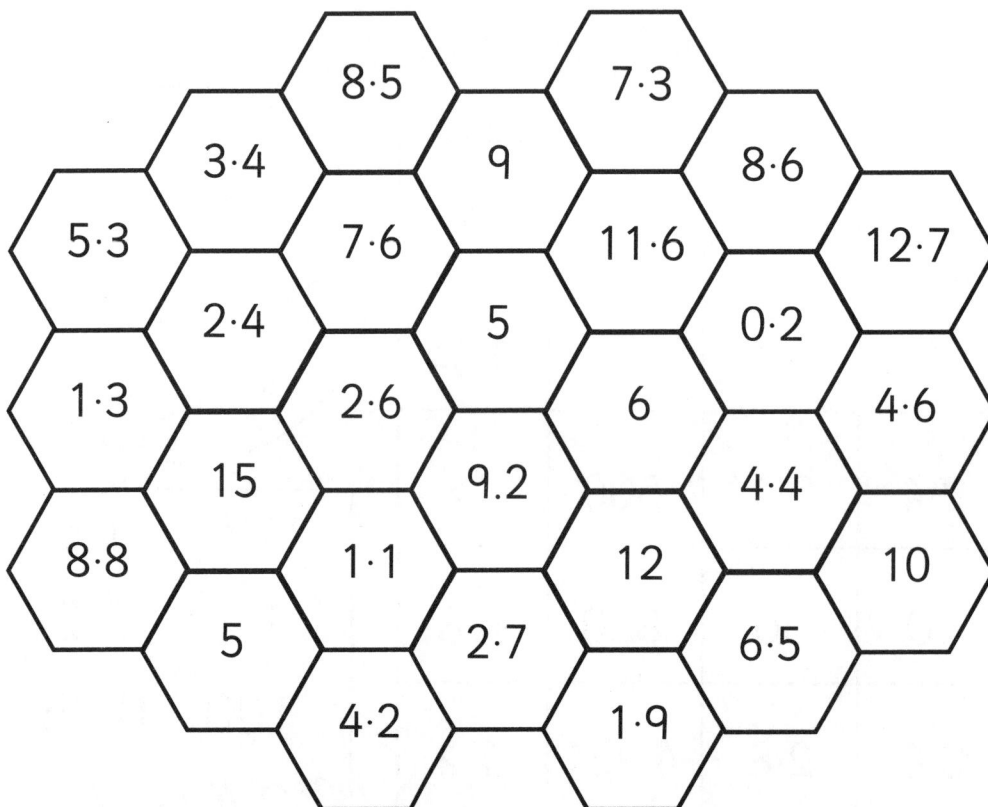

8·5 7·3	
3·4 9 8·6	
5·3 7·6 11·6 12·7	
2·4 5 0·2	
1·3 2·6 6 4·6	
15 9.2 4·4	
8·8 1·1 12 10	
5 2·7 6·5	
4·2 1·9	

A

2	4
0·2	2·4
1·5	5
3	0·7
1·2	9

B

10	2·6
7	5·3
8	7·1
3·7	0·5
0·4	0·6

Name _____   **Date** _____

Book pages

My book is open showing two consecutive page numbers.
When I multiply the two numbers, the answer is 1122.
What are the two numbers? _____

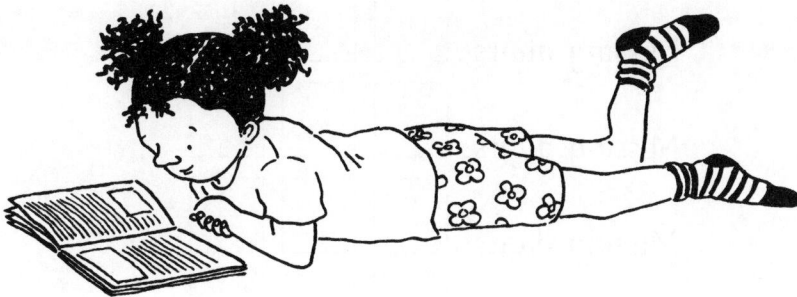

Secret number

Asha chose a number and multiplied it by 4. She then added 4 to it. Finally, she
multiplied the answer by 4 to get the result 2000.
What number did she start with? _____

Name _____ **Date** _____

Virus

1. Johnny's computer developed a virus
and put question marks in the place
of digits on his homework sheet.
What digits are missing?

61 x ?5 = 335?   Missing digits: ☐ ☐

?5 x ?? = 625   Missing digits: ☐ ☐ ☐

8? x 8? = ?400   Missing digits: ☐ ☐ ☐

4? x ?? = 2478   Missing digits: ☐ ☐ ☐

2. Imagine you can only use the keys ③, ④, +, −, = on a calculator.
Make all the numbers from 1 to 10.

Three discs

I have three discs with 9, 8 and 6 written on one side.
Can you work out the numbers on the other side of each
disc from the following clues?

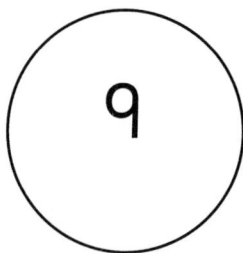

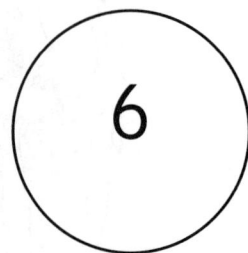

(9)   (8)   (6)

When I flipped the three discs the totals were 23, 12, 13, 15, 16, 19, 20. One of the
numbers on the opposite sides is 2.
Numbers _____

Name _____ **Date** _____

Digit order

Keeping the digits 1 2 3 4 5 6 7 8   9 in order and using signs + and –, how many ways can you make 100?
There are many ways of doing this, one example is given here.

$$1 + 2 + 3 - 4 + 5 + 6 + 78 + 9 = 100$$

Missing values

In the grid the four symbols have different values.
The value of a shape is always the same.
Work out what each symbol means and the missing total.

◯	◯	★	□	32	□ =
◯	◯	◯	◯	24	△ =
△	◯	★	□	?	★ =
★	△	□	□	38	◯ =
34	28	?	30		

Name _____   **Date** _____

Collins Mental Maths © HarperCollins Publishers Ltd 1998

Teacher's Guide – Answers

SECTION 2

Page 11 Hops to the target

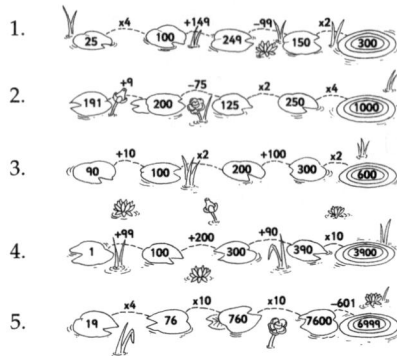

1. 25 →x4→ 100 →+149→ 249 →-99→ 150 →x2→ 300
2. 191 →+9→ 200 →-75→ 125 →x2→ 250 →x4→ 1000
3. 90 →+10→ 100 →x2→ 200 →+100→ 300 →x2→ 600
4. 1 →+99→ 100 →+200→ 300 →+90→ 390 →x10→ 3900
5. 19 →x4→ 76 →x10→ 760 →x10→ 7600 →-601→ 6999

Page 13 Sequence trails

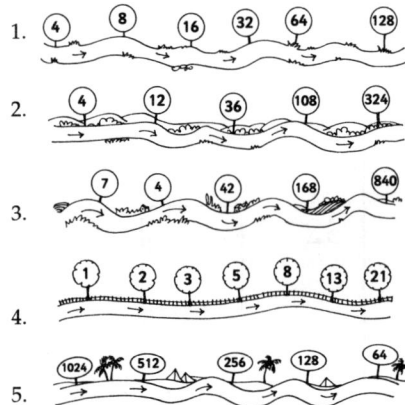

1. 4 → 8 → 16 → 32 → 64 → 128
2. 4 → 12 → 36 → 108 → 324
3. 7 → 4 → 42 → 168 → 840
4. 1 → 2 → 3 → 5 → 8 → 13 → 21
5. 1024 → 512 → 256 → 128 → 64

Page 15 Number machines

Page 17 Rounding luck
The winner was Shanti
Alan circled 50·3
Shanti circled 269 509 16·8 and 998
Winston circled 297 7·8
Melanie circled 117

Page 19 Mysteries
1. 38   2. 760   3. 2110   4. 275

Page 21 Reduce to zero
This page allows children to check their solutions with a calculator which is a valuable visual experience.

Page 23 Decimal trails
3·5   5·5   2·8   7·89   1·5   5·15

Page 25 Jammed

Multiply by 10	Divide by 10
34	0·37
89	3·61
7·0	17·0
12	2·189
113	0·076
126·2	0·199
617·3	0·206

Multiply by 100	Divide by 100
370	0·0476
130	0·536
778	0·0463
620	0·0098
876	0·1005
83	0·43
1076	0·069

Page 27 The culprit
1. 4851   2. 9216

Page 29 Fast times
27 x 5	99 x 5
63 x 9	69 x 8
47 x 4	83 x 7
83 x 6	48 x 7
56 x 7	
37 x 8	
39 x 9	
77 x 9	

Page 31 Division check
1. P	6. W
2. W	7. P
3. P	8. P
4. W	9. P
5. W	10. W

Page 33 Best fit
1. a	5. a
2. b	6. c
3. c	7. b
4. b	

Page 35 Treasure search
Winning route – £2000 + £ 26 230 + £1000 + £4080 = £33 310

Page 37 Broken keys
Open-ended possibilities

Page 39 Number quiz
1. 7631   6731
   7613   6713   3761
   7361   6371   3716
   7316   6317   3671
2. 114, 133, 152, 171, 190
3. 1189, 1160, 1218, 1131, 1102, 1247
4. 41 and 42
5. 1200
6. 22 x 20p
   22 x 50p
7. 39, 78, 117, 195, 234, 273, 312 and so on
8. 841

Page 41 Grubo's fast food

Matthew	Hassan	Natalie	Asha
88	£1·52	64	£1·28
51	£1·02	76	£1·02
50	28	£1·02	42
56	50	28	50
£2·45	£3·32	£2·70	£3·22

Hassan and Asha cannot afford to order their chosen food

Page 43 Digits search
1. 18	6. 3, 5
2. 29	7. 5
3. 32	8. 25
4. 3	9. 2
5. 12	10. 3

Puzzle 1 Amazing
1. 975 + 864 = 1839
2. 234 – 198 = 36
3. 986 x 75 = 73 950
4. 123 ÷ 9 = 13 r 6
5. 987 ÷ 12 = 82 r 3
6. 234 x 1 = 234
7. several possibilities

Puzzle 2 Cross number

a.1	4	b.4	c.3	8	d.7
1	e.2	7	4	f.1	2
g.6	3	9	3	h.2	4
i.1	4	0	j.2	5	k.6
l.2	m.4	0	n.3	o.7	2
0	p.7	0	2	q.2	5

Puzzle 3 Quick match
1. 961	4. 130
2. 599 + 600 + 601	5. 1001
3. 8100	6. 27 x 28

Puzzle 9
Book pages – 33 and 34
Secret number – 124

Puzzle 10
Virus
61 x 55 = 3355
25 x 25
80 x 80 = 6400
42 x 59

Calculator fun – several possibilities

Three discs
9 8 6
2 7 3

Puzzle 10
Digit order - several possibilities

Missing values
☐ = 8   △ = 10   ★ = 12   ○ = 6

Missing numbers = 38 and 36

Answers

PUPIL BOOK 5

Page 2
Making 100
1. 73
2. 57
3. 39
4. 83
5. 62
6. 46
7. 18
8. 65
9. 24
10. 9
11. 69
12. 28
13. 52
14. 71
15. 47

Making 1000
1. 640
2. 460
3. 880
4. 330
5. 810
6. 260
7. 70
8. 790
9. 550
10. 930
11. 320
12. 130
13. 410
14. 280
15. 770

Page 3
Making 10
1. 6·3
2. 5·1
3. 3·2
4. 2·9
5. 1·5
6. 7·7
7. 4·6
8. 8·2
9. 0·8
10. 2·4
11. 9·3
12. 5·1
13. 2·7
14. 8·5
15. 9·1

Number sequences
1. 73, 84
2. 3700, 4200
3. 36, 49
4. 0, 2
5. 33, 51
6. 88, 126
7. −15, −12
8. 160, 320
9. 121, 110, 88, 77
10. 211, 202
11. 1, 6
12. 505, 512
13. 1210, 1430
14. 9900, 10 200
15. 56, 45

Page 4
Doubles and halves
to 99 + 99
1. 76
2. 31 + 31
3. 110
4. 43 + 43
5. 146
6. 172
7. 49 + 49
8. 72 + 72
9. 192

10. 91 + 91
11. 68 + 68
12. 158
13. 132
14. 58 + 58
15. 96 + 96

Doubles and halves of
multiples of 10
1. 740
2. 1160
3. 1380
4. 490 + 490
5. 740 + 740
6. 1720
7. 510 + 510
8. 370 + 370
9. 1180
10. 1700
11. 660 + 660
12. 990 + 990
13. 1360
14. 1860
15. 840 + 840

Page 5
Doubles and halves of
multiples of 100
1. 7800
2. 9400
3. 4300 + 4300
4. 11 000
5. 6100
6. 5400
7. 14 800
8. 13 200
9. 7300 + 7300
10. 7900 + 7900
11. 15 400
12. 17 800
13. 8200 + 8200
14. 9800 + 9800
15. 19 000

Adding 3 numbers
1. 105
2. 113
3. 108
4. 78
5. 108
6. 119
7. 116
8. 119
9. 101
10. 134
11. 114
12. 135
13. 75
14. 115
15. 107

Page 6
Strategies
1. 464
2. 424
3. 518
4. 396
5. 160
6. 220
7. 434
8. 429
9. 641
10. 757
11. 811
12. 711
13. 321
14. 190
15. 552

Adding and
subtracting 9s
1. 366

2. 160
3. 492
4. 747
5. 374
6. 714
7. 207
8. 634
9. 407
10. 605
11. 235
12. 417
13. 698
14. 637
15. 359

Page 7
Adding and
subtracting 11, 21, 31...
1. 368
2. 620
3. 238
4. 406
5. 587
6. 245
7. 595
8. 692
9. 222
10. 866
11. 757
12. 526
13. 692
14. 294
15. 758

Check up 1
1. 530
2. 71
3. 110
4. 17
5. 5·9
6. 6800
7. 1440
8. 367
9. 309
10. 6·9
11. 787
12. 178
13. 107
14. 29
15. 36 000

Page 8
Rounding
1. 370
2. 1000
3. 4240
4. 2000
5. 7010
6. 800
7. 1000
8. 4000
9. 3900
10. 9000
11. 2000
12. 5000
13. 7000
14. 9000
15. 10 000

The nearest hundred
1. 652
2. 175
3. 974
4. 856
5. 127
6. 987
7. 635
8. 39
9. 932
10. 133
11. 984
12. 69
13. 146
14. 776
15. 423

Page 9
The nearest thousand
1. 3679
2. 583
3. 9008
4. 7641
5. 2012
6. 3688
7. 9223
8. 13 314

9. 1919
10. 8367
11. 1321
12. 313
13. 3104
14. 9789
15. 7505

Adding and
subtracting three-digit
multiples of 10
1. 760
2. 270
3. 270
4. 490
5. 510
6. 480
7. 740
8. 590
9. 460
10. 270
11. 900
12. 340
13. 560
14. 340
15. 650

Page 10
Adding and
subtracting multiples
of 100
1. 1200
2. 1800
3. 1100
4. 300
5. 700
6. 300
7. 900
8. 1600
9. 300
10. 800
11. 700
12. 700
13. 800

More than a thousand
1. 1158
2. 847
3. 1225
4. 799
5. 900
6. 831
7. 8238
8. 859
9. 500
10. 812
11. 800
12. 1676
13. 800
14. 897
15. 722

Page 11
Adding and
subtracting three-digit
numbers
1. 983
2. 347
3. 989
4. 328
5. 430
6. 210
7. 877
8. 998
9. 222
10. 779
11. 110
12. 730
13. 724
14. 510
15. 544

Making hundreds
1. 41
2. 22
3. 11
4. 48
5. 76
6. 64
7. 91
8. 87
9. 59
10. 75
11. 49
12. 67
13. 276

14. 82
15. 48

Page 12
What's the difference?
1. 12
2. 123
3. 12
4. 5022
5. 2034
6. 5010
7. 8005
8. 16
9. 6979
10. 3026
11. 8124
12. 112
13. 106
14. 5009
15. 2983

Making whole
numbers
1. 0·8
2. 0·8
3. 0·4
4. 0·9
5. 0·1
6. 0·3
7. 0·2
8. 0·5
9. 0·6
10. 0·7
11. 0·9
12. 0·4
13. 0·8
14. 0·5
15. 0·7

Page 13
Adding and
subtracting tenths
1. 9·8
2. 6·3
3. 2·3
4. 2·6
5. 3·3
6. 2·2
7. 6·1
8. 3·4
9. 5·8
10. 1·6
11. 2·6
12. 4·4
13. 1·6
14. 8·5
15. 0·6

Adding and
subtracting tenths and
hundredths
1. 0·12
2. 1·01
3. 0·24
4. 0·27
5. 1·64
6. 0·04
7. 0·92
8. 0·11
9. 0·37
10. 0·18
11. 0·08
12. 0·84
13. 8·8
14. 0·31
15. 0·25

Page 14
More number
sequences
1. 2·0, 2·2
2. 1, 0·7
3. 3, 3·25
4. 3·45, 3·67
5. 5·7, 6·2
6. 8, 8·2

Ordering decimals
1. 5·23, 3·52, 3·25, 2·35,
2. 1·9 m, 1·19 m, 1·09 m, 0·91 m, 0·19 m
3. 10·33, 10·3, 10·13, 10·03
4. 4·98 g, 4·78 g, 4·58 g, 3·89 g, 2·79 g,
5. 4·4, 4·14, 4·04, 1·14, 0·04

6. 9·94, 9·79, 9·36, 8·84, 6·89,

Check up 2
1. 0·72
2. 8
3. 0·4
4. 19
5. 10·1
6. 180
7. 800
8. 6927
9. 877
10. 8168
11. 24
12. 2·3
13. 2989
14. 0·36
15. 53

Page 15
Multiplication and
division facts 1
1. 32
2. 4
3. 42
4. 7
5. 9
6. 5
7. 4
8. 27
9. 36
10. 12
11. 9
12. 0
13. 5
14. 7
15. 10

Multiplication and
division facts 2
1. 4
2. 72
3. 0
4. 18
5. 9
6. 8
7. 100
8. 8
9. 9
10. 5
11. 7
12. 54
13. 6
14. 5
15. 32

Page 16
Doubling and halving
odd numbers to 100
1. 13·5
2. 20·5
3. 27·5
4. 95
5. 39
6. 29½
7. 51
8. 39½
9. 31½
10. 95
11. 43½
12. 45½
13. 79
14. 91
15. 38½

Doubling and halving
odd multiples of 10
1. 650
2. 245
3. 185
4. 375
5. 187½
6. 245
7. 970
8. 275
9. 370
10. 245
11. 355
12. 247½
13. 530
14. 460
15. 155

Page 17
Doubling and halving odd multiples of 100
1. 2150
2. 850
3. 6500
4. 2450
5. 3550
6. 8700
7. 5700
8. 3450
9. 4050
10. 7100
11. 4600
12. 2100
13. 3750
14. 7900
15. 4950

Mixed doubles and halves
1. 9
2. £1.75
3. $47\frac{1}{2}$
4. 50 cm
5. 39
6. 360
7. 490
8. £6.17
9. 685
10. 0·7 m
11. £11.50
12. $41\frac{1}{2}$ cm
13. 91
14. 500 m
15. 150

Page 18
Doubling and halving the result
1. 210
2. 115
3. 135
4. 360
5. 185
6. 455
7. 195
8. 710
9. 280
10. 495
11. 270
12. 240
13. 1370
14. 315
15. 495

Halving and doubling the result
1. 1040
2. 210
3. 198
4. 272
5. 144
6. 1780
7. 576
8. 294
9. 242
10. 216
11. 2880
12. 976
13. 136
14. 208
15. 162

Page 19
Check up 3
1. 35
2. 90
3. 245
4. 48
5. 63
6. $46\frac{1}{2}$
7. 176
8. 5 x 5
9. 790
8. 7
9. $39\frac{1}{2}$
10. 3150
11. 610
12. 9700
13. $46\frac{1}{2}$

Multiplying by 50
1. 1200
2. 1650

3. 4300
4. 850
5. 2150
6. 21
7. 44
8. 57
9. 2950
10. 3600
11. 5200
12. 63
13. 84
14. 29
15. 1950

Page 20
Double and double again
1. 15, 30, 60, 120, 240, 480
2. 75, 150, 300, 600, 1200, 2400
3. 180, 360, 720, 1440, 2880, 5760
4. 13, 26, 52, 104, 208, 416
5. 77, 154, 308, 616, 1232, 2464
6. 35, 70, 140, 280, 560, 1120

Page 21
The 14 times table
1. 84
2. 56
3. 126
4. 70
5. 112
6. 98

The 16 times table
1. 48
2. 144
3. 112
4. 80
5. 64
6. 128

Finding fractions by doubling and halving
1. 12
2. 5
3. 8
4. 13
5. 21
6. 12
7. 35
8. 48
9. 62
10. 29
11. 54
12. 72

Page 22
The 12 times table
1. 156
2. 216
3. 264
4. 372
5. 180
6. 300
7. 516
8. 612
9. 204
10. 324
11. 228
12. 420
13. 360
14. 252
15. 192

Multiplying by 21
1. 189
2. 273
3. 357
4. 462
5. 231
6. 651
7. 147
8. 336
9. 525
10. 378
11. 168
12. 294
13. 399
14. 126

14. 840

Page 23
Multiplying by 19
1. 133
2. 285
3. 418
4. 95
5. 209
6. 152
7. 570
8. 323
9. 171
10. 247
11. 361
12. 114
13. 304
14. 380
15. 342

Multiplying two-digit numbers
1. 252
2. 216
3. 279
4. 364
5. 252
6. 225
7. 288
8. 203
9. 285
10. 387
11. 330
12. 190
13. 222
14. 280
15. 402

Page 24
Related facts
1. 18
2. 17
3. 13
4. 14
5. 18
6. 18
7. 17
8. 13
9. 14
10. 15
11. 18
12.
a. 360 ÷ 12 = 30
   360 ÷ 30 = 12
   12 x 30 = 360
   30 x 12 = 360
b. 375 ÷ 15 = 25
   375 ÷ 25 = 15
   15 x 25 = 375
   25 x 15 = 375
c. 356 ÷ 19 = 24
   356 ÷ 24 = 19
   19 x 24 = 356
   24 x 19 = 356
d. 600 ÷ 40 = 15
   600 ÷ 15 = 40
   40 x 15 = 600
   15 x 40 = 600

Check up 4
1. 273
2. 2200
3. 204
4. 32, 64, 128, 16 x 16 = 256, 32 x 16 = 512
5. 96
6. 13 x 19 = 247
7. 171
8. 50
9. 285
10. 3
11. 276
12. 6
13. 504
14. 182
15. 552 ÷ 24 = 23
    552 ÷ 23 = 24
    23 x 24 = 552
    24 x 23 = 552

Page 25
Multiplying multiples of 10 by multiples of 100
1. 24 000

2. 28 000
3. 900
4. 24 000
5. 24 000
6. 700
7. 72 000
8. 900
9. 63 000
10. 60
11. 64 000
12. 40
13. 21 000
14. 40
15. 900

Dividing by 10, 100 or 1000
1. 62
2. 300
3. 7
4. 500
5. 2300
6. 100
7. 4000
8. 2000
9. 40
10. 6000
11. 100
12. 75
13. 8000
14. 3000
15. 700 000

Page 26
Multiplying tens and hundreds by a single digit
1. 3000
2. 7
3. 600
4. 450
5. 70
6. 7
7. 180
8. 7
9. 2
10. 80
11. 150
12. 560
13. 50
14. 6
15. 320

Two operations
1. 300
2. 290
3. 600
4. 7
5. 4500
6. 20
7. 180
8. 800
9. 200
10. 70
11. 600
12. 8
13. 90
14. 1
15. 900

Page 27
Factors
1. 1, 2, 3, 6, 9, 18
2. 1, 2, 3, 5, 6, 10, 15, 30
3. 1, 3, 5, 9, 15, 45
4. 1, 2, 3, 4, 6, 8, 12, 24
5. 1, 2, 4, 7, 8, 14, 28, 56
6. 1, 3, 7, 9, 21, 63
7. 1, 17
8. 1, 2, 3, 4, 6, 12
9. 1, 2, 4, 5, 10, 20, 25, 50, 100
10. 1, 2, 4, 8, 16, 32, 64
11. 1, 5, 15, 75
12. 1, 7, 49
13. 1, 3, 9, 11, 33, 99
14. 1, 57
15. 1, 29

Using factors to multiply and divide
1. 138
2. 261
3. 272
4. 114

2. 216
3. 369
4. 12
5. 14
6. 14
7. 13
8. 21
9. 54

Page 28
Divisibility tests
1. true
2. true
3. false
4. true
5. false
6. true
7. true
8. true
9. false
10. false
11. 246
12. 504
13. true
14. false
15. false
16. true
17. 506, 517, 528, 539, 550, 561, 572, 583, 594

Page 29
Square numbers and prime numbers
1. 64
2. 36
3. 10
4. 144
5. 15
6. 11
7. 81
8. 13
9. 49
10. 25
11. 23, 43, 53
12. 11, 13, 17, 19
13. 31, 37, 41, 43
14. 51, 53, 57, 59, 61, 67
15. 87, 89, 91, 97

Percentages
1. £9
2. 6 m
3. 180
4. £60
5. 15p
6. 6
7. 5p
8. 210 g
9. 24p
10. 24
11. 600 ml
12. 21p
13. 55 %
14. 68 %
15. 43 %

Page 30
Fractions
1. 12
2. 20p
3. 8
4. $66\frac{3}{4}$
5. 100 m
6. 53p
7. 35 cm
8. 90
9. $2\frac{1}{4}, 2\frac{1}{2}, 2\frac{3}{4}, 3, 3\frac{1}{4}$,
10. $1\frac{1}{10}, 1\frac{3}{10}, 1\frac{1}{2}, 2, 2\frac{1}{10}$
11. $1\frac{3}{4}$ litres
12. $\frac{3}{8}, \frac{2}{8}$
13. $5\frac{1}{3}$
14. $1\frac{1}{4}$
15. $\frac{7}{20}, \frac{4}{5}$

Money
1. 20p
2. 40p
3. 85p
4. 90p
5. £4.50
6. £4.50
7. 35p
8. £7.52
9. £14.01

10. £18.77
11. 1150
12. 200
13. 89
14. £2.50
15. 160

Page 31
Measures
1. 350 cm
2. 10 000
3. 7200 g
4. 4300 mm
5. 23 000 000
6. $\frac{1}{4}$
7. $\frac{3}{4}$
8. $\frac{1}{10}$
9. 73 cm
10. 0·7 km
11. −24 960
12. 7·7

Time
1. 120
2. 140
3. 480
4. 900
5. 730
6. 150
7. 720
8. 2000
9. 40 minutes
10. 1 hour 25 minutes
11. 12 minutes
12. 19:05
13. 20:05
14. 21:00

Page 32
Check up 5
1. £1
2. true
3. 90
4. 500 m
5. 70
6. £0.72
6. 1, 2, 4, 8, 16, 32
7. 121
8. 3p
9. 100
10. 15 000
11. 192
12. 13
13. £2.62
14. 23, 29, 31, 37

Check up 6
1. 10:50 p.m.
2. 160 m
3. 35
4. 203
5. £5.44
6. 0·31
7. 7 degrees
8. 100
9. 3024 m
10. 16 cm

Answers

PUPIL BOOK 6

Page 2
Rounding to the
nearest 10, 100 or 1000
1. 90
2. 350
3. 12 010
4. 34 900
5. 65 990 or 66 000
6. 600
7. 10 500
8. 29 700
9. 79 000
10. 20 000
11. 5000
12. 23 000
13. 49 000
14. 70 000
15. 99 000

Rounding decimals
1. 3
2. 5
3. 13
4. 29
5. 38
6. 130
7. 500
8. 27·8
9. 34·7
10. 12·7 or 12·8
11. 211·9
12. 65
13. 477·1
14. 321·1
15. 50

Page 3
Number sequences
1. 98, 117
2. −19, −8, 3
3. 36, 49
4. 204, 229
5. 53, 23
6. 21, 34, 55, 89
7. 10, 1
8. 1, 1·3
9. 28, 36
10. 180, 159
11. 7, −2, −11
12. 0·43, 0·47
13. 39 700, 40 000
14. 60 219, 59 219

Ordering numbers
1. −29, −19,−8, 18, 21
2. 19, 199, 19 091, 19 919,
    19 991, 19 0991
3. −7, −5, −2, 2, 5, 7
4. 205 000, 225 000,
    250 000, 275 000, 285 000
5. 17·17, 17·7, 17·71, 71·17,
    71·7
6. 4·56, 4·64, 5·46, 5·64,
    6.45

Negative numbers
1. −9°C
2. 2°C
3. 8°C
4. 16°C
5. 16°C
6. −10°C

Page 4
Squares and cubes
1. 64
2. 4
3. 11
4. 225
5. 9
6. 244
7. 27
8. 10
9. 729

Factors and prime factors
1. 1, 2, 3, 4, 6, 8, 12, 24
2. 1, 2, 4, 13, 26, 52
3. 1, 5, 25, 125
4. 1, 3, 9, 11, 33, 99
5. 1, 2, 4, 5, 8, 10, 20, 25,
    40, 50, 100, 125, 250,
    200, 500, 1000
6. 25
7. 5, 17, 64, 61
8. 3, 7
9. 17
10. 7
11. 67
12. 3
13. 3
14. 89
15.

Page 5
Multiples
1. true
2. true
3. false
4. true
5. false
6. false
7. false
8. true
9. 6
10. 15
11. 3
12. 6
13. 25
14. 3
15. 8

Check up 1
1. 64
2. 1, 2, 4, 5, 10, 20, 25, 50,
    100, 125, 250, 500
3. 80 000
4. 13
5. 33, 39, 45
6. 3, 27
7. 29·43, 29·34, 24·93,
    24·39, 23·94,
8. 100
9. 112, 70
10. 39
11. 12
12. 26°C

Page 6
Fractions
1. 5
2. 15
3. 21
4. 51
5. 5
6. 18
7. 37
8. 62
9. 6
10. 16
11. 32
12. 37
13. $1\frac{1}{4}$, $1\frac{4}{5}$, $2\frac{1}{2}$ $2\frac{5}{8}$, $2\frac{2}{3}$
14. $4\frac{1}{4}$, $4\frac{3}{10}$, $5\frac{1}{2}$, $5\frac{3}{4}$, $5\frac{7}{10}$
15. 6
16. 27
17. 24
18. 60
19. 700
20. 21
21. 55
22. 70
23. 160
24. 40
25. $\frac{3}{4}$
26. $\frac{3}{5}$
27. $\frac{7}{8}$
28. $\frac{91}{100}$
29. $3\frac{3}{8}$
30. $6\frac{1}{2}$
31. $\frac{9}{20}$
32. $1\frac{1}{5}$

33. $\frac{11}{40}$
34. $\frac{3}{4}$
35. $\frac{1}{8}$

Page 7
Percentages
1. 35 m
2. 15p
3. 225
4. 6 kg
5. £1.80
6. swimming costume:
    £1.20 off; new price
    £10.80 socks: 26p off;
    new price £2.34
7. trainers: £5.40 off;
    £21.60
8. tennis racket: £8 off;
    new price £24
    T-shirt: £11.25 off; new
    price £33.75
9. £4.20
10. £3.15
11. 63p
12. £21
13. £4.97
14. 6 matches
15. 12 children

Page 8
Making 10, 100 or 1000
1. 29
2. 5·2
3. 326
4. 718
5. 8·3
6. 37
7. 6·6
8. 55
9. 632
10. 9·2
11. 889
12. 61
13. 7·8
14. 83
15. 56

Mixed doubles
and halves
1. 178
2. 1520
3. 3200
4. 800
5. 1580
6. 7000
7. 152
8. 66
9. 9400
10. 48
11. 17 600
12. 390
13. 270
14. 3400
15. 9900

Page 9
Near doubles
1. 154
2. 3100
3. 560
4. 177
5. 1110
6. 9700
7. 15 300
8. 1910
9. 52
10. 720
11. 15 600
12. 137
13. 540
14. 196
15. 19 600

Check up 2
1. 134
2. 653
3. 22
4. 710
5. 120
6. 1900
7. 26
8. 3·3
9. 173
10. £43.75
11. $3\frac{2}{5}$, $3\frac{3}{4}$, $3\frac{9}{10}$, $4\frac{1}{3}$
12. 537
13. 9800
14. £280
15. 29

Page 10
Counting up
1. 695

2. 431
3. 508
4. 832
5. 609
6. 819
7. 331
8. 2624
9. 2319
10. 4965
11. 1796
12. 4372
13. 1563
14. 5684
15. 1638

Partitioning
1. 475
2. 831
3. 818
4. 786
5. 933
6. 441
7. 851
8. 371
9. 243
10. 619
11. 582
12. 475
13. 562
14. 516
15. 416

Page 11
Adding several
two-digit numbers
1. 105
2. 206
3. 27
4. 22
5. 200
6. 97
7. 22
8. 155
9. 88
10. 113
11. 290
12. 98
13. 18
14. 40
15. 167

Adding several
three-digit numbers
1. 750
2. 1380
3. 140
4. 310
5. 1000
6. 180
7. 150
8. 230
9. 160
10. 2220
11. 1080
12. 630
13. 170
14. 850
15. 1930

Page 12
Adding and subtracting
four-digit multiples
of 100
1. 7300
2. 2910
3. 2700
4. 3800
5. 3800
6. 5900
7. 2900
8. 8100
9. 8700
10. 9300
11. 4400
12. 700
13. 1800
14. 8000
15. 4600

Adding and subtracting
multiples of 10
1. 917
2. 170
3. 775
4. 1012
5. 471
6. 251
7. 263
8. 1236
9. 472
10. 287
11. 244
12. 1198

13. 291
14. 1047
15. 9121

Page 13
Related facts – whole
numbers
1. 4710
    1230 + 3480 = 4710
    4710 − 1230 = 3480
    4710 − 3480 = 1230
2. 1550
    4420 − 1550 = 2870
    1550 + 2870 = 4420
    2870 + 1550 = 4420
3. 5930
    4680 + 1250 = 5930
    5930 − 4680 = 1250
    5930 − 1250 = 4680
4. 2480
    9840 − 2480 = 7360
    2480 + 7360 = 9840
    7360 + 2480 = 7360
5. 3280
    6710 − 3280 = 3430
    3280 + 3430 = 6710
    3430 + 3280 = 6710
6. 3760
    5000 − 3760 = 1240
    1240 + 3760 = 5000
    3760 + 1240 = 5000
7. 6300
    750 + 5550 = 6300
    6300 − 750 = 5550
    6300 − 5550 = 750
8. 6250
    2570 + 3680 = 6250
    6250 − 3680 = 2570
    6250 − 2570 = 3680
9. 1250
    4200 − 1250 = 2950
    1250 + 2950 = 4200
    2950 + 1250 = 4200
10. 9290
    1870 + 7420 = 9290
    9290 − 7420 = 1870
    9290 − 1870 = 7420
11. 1800 + 3800 = 5600
    3800 + 1800 = 5600
    5600 − 1800 = 3800
    5600 − 3800 = 1800
12. 1860 + 1890 = 3750
    1890 + 1860 = 3750
    3750 − 1860 = 1890
    3750 − 1890 = 1860
13. 3200 + 3210 = 6410
    3210 + 3200 = 6410
    6410 − 3210 = 3200
    6410 − 3200 = 3210
14. 4350 + 3560 = 7910
    3560 + 4350 = 7910
    7910 − 3560 = 4350
    7910 − 4350 = 3560

Check up 3
1. 2681
2. 83
3. 1600
4. 161
5. 70
6. 93
7. 290
8. 883
9. 1400
10. 2433
11. 832
12. 128
13. 263
14. 8400
15. 109

Page 14
To the next tenth or
whole number
1. 0·54
2. 0·07
3. 0·09
4. 0·67
5. 0·06
6. 0·01
7. 0·89
8. 0·96
9. 0·41
10. 0·08
11. 0·66
12. 0·49
13. 0·07
14. 0·02
15. 0·46

Adding and subtracting
decimals less than 1
1. 0·86

2. 0·61
3. 0·31
4. 0·3
5. 0·52
6. 0·2
7. 0·74
8. 0·31
9. 0·29
10. 0·2
11. 0·28
12. 0·4
13. 0·01
14. 0·11
15. 0·76

Page 15
Adding and subtracting
decimals more than 1
1. 9·72
2. 18·9
3. 2·69
4. 3·41
5. 3·51
6. 2·24
7. 9·66
8. 3·6
9. 10·03
10. 11·68
11. 8·1
12. 14·38
13. 24·59
14. 12·52
15. 11·14

Related facts – decimals
1. 9·09
    3·89 + 5·2 = 9·09
    9·09 − 5·2 = 3·89
    9·09 − 3·89 = 5·2
2. 4·91
    7·43 − 4·91 = 2·51
    4·91 + 2·51 = 7·43
    2·51 + 4·91 = 7·43
3. 3·28
    5·4 − 3·28 = 2·12
    2·12 + 3·28 = 5·4
    3·28 + 2·12 = 5·4
4. 27·92
    15·58 + 12·34 = 27·92
    27·92 − 15·58 = 12·34
    27·92 − 12·34 = 15·58
5. 7·91
    13·81 − 7·91 = 5·9
    7·91 + 5·9 = 13·81
    5·9 + 7·91 = 13·81
6. 10·1
    3·81 + 6·29 = 10·1
    10·1 − 3·81 = 6·29
    10·1 − 6·29 = 3·81
7. 3·23
    31·22 − 3·23 = 27·99
    27·99 + 3·23 = 31·22
    3·23 + 27·99 = 31·22
8. 18·7
    8·95 + 9·75 = 18·7
    18·7 − 9·75 = 8·95
    18·7 − 8·95 = 9·75
9. 2·92
    12·32 − 2·92 = 9·4
    9·4 + 2·92 = 12·32
    2·92 + 9·4 = 12·32
10. 60·6
    24·24 + 36·36 = 60·6
    60·6 − 24·24 = 36·36
    60·6 − 36·36 = 24·24
11. 2·31 + 0·91 = 3·22
    0·91 + 2·31 = 3·22
    3·22 − 0·91 = 2·31
    3·22 − 2·31 = 0·91
12. 7·56 + 7·6 = 15·16
    7·6 + 7·56 = 15·16
    15·16 − 7·56 = 7·6
    15·16 − 7·6 = 7·56
13. 6·31 + 6·33 = 12·64
    6·33 + 6·31 = 12·64
    12·64 − 6·31 = 6·33
    12·64 − 6·33 = 6·31
14. 19·24 + 18·27 = 37·51
    18·27 + 19·24 = 37·51
    37·51 − 18·27 = 19·24
    37·51 − 19·24 = 18·27
15. 7·35 + 7·65 = 15
    7·65 + 7·35 = 15
    15 − 7·65 = 7·35
    15 − 7·35 = 7·65

Page 16
Decimal problems
1. 1·8
2. 0·6
3. 7·5
4. 1·4
5. 6·6

6. 6·7
7. 10·7
8. 4·5
9. 10·8
10. 10·4
11. 2·6
12. 10·8
13. 6·6
14. 29·3

Check up 4
1. 0·03
2. 0·95
3. 0·63
4. 1·9
5. 2·24
6. 4·28
7. 0·3
8. 16·71
9. 0·14
10. 0·09
11. 5·87
12. 35
13. 2·79
14. 0·08
15. 4·8

Page 17
Table facts
1. 48
2. 9
3. 9
4. 27
5. 4
6. 56
7. 9
8. 36
9. 8
10. 42
11. 72
12. 5
13. 40
14. 8
15. 28

More doubles and halves
1. 48
2. 700
3. 85
4. 17 800
5. 1750
6. 29·5
7. 235
8. 78
9. 3650
10. 2500
11. 53
12. 48½
13. 950
14. 305
15. 550

Page 18
Doubling
1. 346
2. 878
3. 378
4. 754
5. 372
6. 714
7. 952
8. 716
9. 764
10. 332
11. 476
12. 752
13. 838
14. 676
15. 358

Double then halve
1. 115
2. 105
3. 315
4. 160
5. 360
6. 210
7. 630
8. 280
9. 240
10. 405
11. 445
12. 330
13. 245
14. 365
15. 485

Page 19
Halve then double
1. 240
2. 136
3. 98

4. 182
5. 520
6. 256
7. 108
8. 126
9. 128
10. 132
11. 760
12. 256
13. 176
14. 294
15. 96

Multiplying by 15
1. 180
2. 315
3. 135
4. 255
5. 480
6. 360
7. 270
8. 405
9. 615
10. 165
11. 375
12. 540
13. 435
14. 450
15. 525

Page 20
Multiplying by 25
1. 400
2. 1120
3. 1100
4. 450
5. 550
6. 850
7. 775
8. 475
9. 525
10. 875
11. 1025
12. 975
13. 425
14. 900
15. 2050

Doubling tables facts
1. 108
2. 112
3. 108
4. 126
5. 84
6. 72
7. 112
8. 84
9. 162
10. 144
11. 144
12. 126
13. 96
14. 98
15. 128

Page 21
The 24 times table
1. 72
2. 168
3. 216
4. 120
5. 192
6. 96
7. 144

Double then double again
1. 24, 48, 96, 16
2. 32, 64, 128, 256, 16

Finding fractions by halving
1. 50
2. 35
3. 50
4. 5
5. 75
6. 65
7. 75
8. £750
9. 75
10. 0·25 m
11. 250
12. 25
13. 15
14. 15
15. 500

Page 22
Check up 5
1. 174
2. 95

3. 210
4. 356
5. 725
6. 5
7. 270
8. 210
9. 238
10. 710
11. 48·5
12. 825
13. 270
14. 35
15. 1175

Using factors
1. 27
2. 567
3. 738
4. 22
5. 352
6. 15
7. 238
8. 304
9. 304
10. 408
11. 21
12. 414

Page 23
The 17 times table
1. 68
2. 119
3. 51
4. 153
5. 102
6. 136
7. 85

Multiplying and dividing by 10, 100 and 1000
1. 5300
2. 15 000
3. 500
4. 1000
5. 65
6. 10
7. 34
8. 120
9. 1000
10. 100
11. 425
12. 340
13. 100
14. 27 000
15. 10
16. 60
17. 2000
18. 5·2
19. 51 200
20. 35

Page 24
Multiplying by 49 or 51
1. 918
2. 1176
3. 1071
4. 1568
5. 2009
6. 969
7. 1377
8. 1519
9. 816
10. 1715
11. 2703
12. 3136
13. 3621
14. 3675
15. 4067

Multiplying by 99 and 101
1. 1683
2. 2424
3. 3168
4. 3838
5. 2079
6. 3333
7. 4554
8. 4949
9. 3737
10. 4257
11. 5252
12. 5445
13. 6237
14. 7272
15. 7821

Page 25
Multiplying two-digit numbers by a single digit

1. 252
2. 258
3. 376
4. 513
5. 396
6. 584
7. 406
8. 702
9. 376
10. 498
11. 483
12. 595
13. 728
14. 462
15. 544

Check up 6
1. 2277
2. 402
3. 100
4. 153
5. 1519
6. 10
7. 468
8. 56 000
9. 10
10. 4343
11. 119
12. 79
13. 1428
14. 406
15. 6633

Page 26
Multiplying decimals less than 1
1. 2·4
2. 2·1
3. 8
4. 4·5
5. 8
6. 0·7
7. 6
8. 4·2
9. 3·2
10. 0·6
11. 3
12. 2·4
13. 0·1
14. 9
15. 3·5

Multiplying units and tenths by a single digit
1. 28·8
2. 28·8
3. 27
4. 39·9
5. 31·2
6. 57·6
7. 58·4
8. 63·7
9. 52·8
10. 38
11. 34
12. 46·9
13. 36·8
14. 47·7
15. 54·4

Page 27
Multiplying decimals by 10
1. 33·4
2. 41·5
3. £52·20
4. 50·9
5. £68
6. 73·1
7. 35·5
8. 59
9. 4·30 m
10. 80·1
11. 71 kg
12. 10·1
13. 69·2
14. 20·7 m
15. 98·9

Multiplying decimals by 100
1. 610
2. 380
3. £510
4. 8900
5. 370 cm
6. 130
7. 690
8. 420
9. £799
10. 340 cm
11. 470

12. 380
13. £2.90
14. 970
15. 860

Page 28
Dividing decimals by 10 and 100
1. 0·32
2. 4·5
3. 9
4. 0·08
5. 55p
6. 40
7. 0·43
8. 100
9. 10
10. 0·7
11. 0·4
12. 0·09
13. 63
14. 10
15. 100

More related facts – decimals
1. 2·76
2. 2·3
3. 2·3
4. 51·6
5. 4·3
6. 12
7. 15
   6 x 2·5 = 15
   15 ÷ 6 = 2·5
   15 ÷ 2·5 = 6
8. 0·62
   1·24 ÷ 0·62 = 2
   2 x 0·62 = 1·24
   0·62 x 2 = 1·24
9. 0·25
   0·5 ÷ 0·25 = 2
   2 x 0·25 = 0·5
   0·25 x 2 = 0·5
10. 3·69
   203 x 1·23 = 3·60
   3·69 ÷ 1·23 = 3
   3·69 ÷ 3 = 1·23
11. 3·5
   5 x 0·7 = 3·5
   3·5 ÷ 0·7 = 5
   3·5 ÷ 5 = 0·7
12. 0·2 x 0·4 = 0·08
   0·4 x 0·2 = 0·08
   0·08 ÷ 0·4 = 0·2
   0·08 ÷ 0·2 = 0·4

Page 29
Doubling decimals
1. 1·4
2. 0·46
3. 0·14
4. 0·08
5. 0·38
6. 1·3
7. 0·9
8. 1·18
9. 1·34
10. 0·61
11. 0·18
12. 1·2
13. 0·65
14. 0·96
15. 0·87

Halving decimals
1. 0·2
2. 0·34
3. 0·38
4. 0·26
5. 0·34
6. 0·8
7. 0·4
8. 0·78
9. 0·6
10. 0·125
11. 0·15
12. 0·315
13. 0·49
14. 0·355
15. 0·015

Page 30
Check up 7
1. 18·8
2. 50
3. 0·045
4. 1·3
5. 60·5
6. 0·9
7. 100
8. 0·36

9. 10
10. 1·78
11. 4·3
12. 100
13. 19
14. 0·17
15. 3·31

What operation?
1. 345 + 245 = 590
2. 450 x 10 = 4500
3. 475 ÷ 25 = 19
4. 17 – 3 + 10 = 24
5. 107 ÷ 25 = 4·28
6. 107 – 309 = –182
7. 36 ÷ 4 x 7 = 63
8. (18 + 34) ÷ 2 = 26
9. 17 – (15 ÷ 5) = 14
10. 362 x 28 = 10 136
11. 47 – 24 x 4 = 92
12. (96 ÷ 32) + 49 = 52
13. 759 ÷ 25 = 30·36
14. 35 x 3 – 20 = 85
15. (12 – 4) x 14 = 112

Page 31
Money
1. £1.77
2. £1.42
3. £2.70
4. £66.50
5. £9.99
6. 88p
7. £775
8. £124.49
9. £211.60
10. £2.14
11. £2.06
12. £7.36

Time
1. 329
2. 408
3. 3060
4. 1825
5. 1200
6. 92
7. 122
8. 375 miles
9. 21 km
10. 125 minutes
11. 8 hours 35 minutes
12. 3 hours 37 minutes
13. 4 hours 35 minutes
14. 10 hours 44 minutes
15. 1 hour 39 minutes

Page 32
Measures
1. 4500 m
2. 13 000 grams
3. 7000 mm
4. 237 cm
5. 20 000 dm
6. 50 ml
7. 5 oz
8. 48 km
9. 1 lb
10. 1250 ml
11. 0·03 m
12. 0·6 kg
13. 0·34 ml
14. 30·4 m
15. 14 km